You Gotta Start Somewhere

Somewhere

A Weekly Challenge to Get You Started on Life's Greatest Journey

By

Roy D. Mason

Printed in the United States of America

ISBN 978-0-9960417-2-0

The CORE Training, Inc.
9723 Northcross Center Court
Huntersville, NC 28078

Visit our website at www.thecoretraining.com

DEDICATION

This book is dedicated to the love of my life, Mary. I knew from the time I met you in the sixth grade that you were the one for me. I am so thankful that you agreed to marry me in 1978 and remember, as I told you then, "You can leave anytime you want, but I'm going with you!" I love you, Maw-Maw.

To my CORE family:

I met Roy about six years ago and he's changed my life more than any of my previous 11 mentors. He's taught me the lesson of generosity, which has in turn brought me a bounty in my life of clients, friends and love of family. I believe without the lesson of generosity, all we are is a bunch of people focused only on ourselves, whether that be making more money or accumulating more possessions. We are not focused on what really matters, on changing the world by becoming better people in all areas of our lives.

If you truly want to change your life, you have to surround yourself with people that live the life you want to lead. I spend four to six hours a week with Roy, and he has taught me so much about being a better man, a better husband, and a better leader.

Read this book and follow along as I will. Each week has a space for you to journal about areas in your life where you can be more generous, gracious, and grateful. Journaling is very difficult for me, but it is worth the effort. I believe that completing the journaling each week will make all of us better people.
Therefore, I am committed to filling out this book.

Enjoy your life!

Rick Ruby
Majority Partner and Head Coach,
The CORE Training, Inc.
October 2016

ACKNOWLEDGEMENTS

As I sit here, I am so mindful and thankful for the many people who have brought me to this place. I am thankful for those who have prodded me, encouraged me, and believed that I should write this book.

I want to thank Mack Kearney who took me under his wing and taught me to "do the work of the evangelist" around the globe.

I want to thank Jerry Dockery who has been a trusted colleague and friend in the ministry for many years. His insight and leadership are unsurpassed.

I want to thank Rick Ruby and The CORE Training, staff for believing in me and encouraging me to write this book. Rick has made me a better leader and communicator by entrusting me to be a part of his life and work.

I want to thank Trent McCranie for painstakingly editing and helping me with this manuscript. Some of my original work was poorly written and he was gracious and generous with his time and skills.

I want to thank Jeff Andler for the past 15 years of life, love, and leadership. We have spent intense time together traveling around the globe to share the gospel with people. His influence on my life has been the most meaningful of any person I know other than my wife. It was Jeff who most inspired me to write this book.

Most of all I want to thank the Lord Jesus for saving me and giving me the certain hope of eternal life and calling me into full-time ministry where I can unashamedly share His life-changing message with all who will hear.

INTRODUCTION

Wherever you are in life, it's not too late to get on track to a more fulfilled, faithful, and meaningful life. Once you make up your mind to see a change in your character, commitment, and connections in life, you will experience wonderful results. The hardest thing of all is deciding that you want to change.

Everyone is busy. In this face-paced race we call life it is important to keep things in perspective. Far too many people view this race in terms of a sprint, but we should know it as a marathon. We are all in the race and on this journey together. We all strive to be better tomorrow than we are today and because of this, we try to carefully plan our steps.

While walking on this path, it is vitally important to get to where we are going, but it is also important to know that we take the steps one at a time. It is my prayer that as you read this book you will find the single greatest truth in life, which is the fact that God loves you and has a marvelously wonderful plan which includes you!

None of us are perfect, in fact, just the opposite is true. We are flawed: *"But God demonstrates His own love toward us, in that while we were yet sinners, Christ died for us"* (Romans 5:8).

With this as the starting point, I hope you will embrace and accept this "One-A-Week Challenge" and remember, you gotta start somewhere.

THE "ONE-A-WEEK CHALLENGE"

Most people agree to the value of introducing positive thoughts and attitudes into their daily life. Some people look for motivational video clips, or pithy quips that will hopefully equip them to face the day.

Throughout my life I have discovered that the greatest thing we can put into our hearts and minds is the Word of God.

Remember... **Whatever is in the well, comes up in the bucket!** Our heart is a sponge and soaks up whatever is poured into it. Our life will constantly produce the things that we put into our heart. When I soak up the things of the world and the flesh into my heart, then I will spew forth those same things when I speak. I must be careful to pour into my heart the truth of God's word and His character. David wrote, *"I have hidden [treasured] your word in my heart, that I might not sin against you [God]"* (Psalm 119:11 NLT).

It is my prayer that this devotional book will be an aid into introducing you to a simple and systematized approach to ingesting the Word of God. I hope that our wells will be full of the Word of God so that whenever you look into your bucket you will see only the crystal clear water of God's word.

To this end, I want to encourage you to join me in what I am calling the "**One-A-Week**" challenge. This is how it works. There are fifty-two verses of scripture in this book. Throughout the week we will think about the verse and commit it to memory. By this time next year, you will have 52 verses of scripture in your "well" that you will be able to draw upon all the time!

Here are some long-held ideas about the best way to memorize scripture:

1. **Be intentional. Write** the verse on an index card. I know we are in a digital age, but I promise you that by physically writing the verse out on a card you will be able to more quickly memorize it. Besides, at the end of the year you will have 26 cards (a verse on the front and back of each card) that you will cherish in the years to come.

2. **Be involved. Find** the verse in your Bible. When you find the verse, use a highlighter to mark it on the actual pages of your Bible.

3. **Be deliberate. Set aside** a few moments each day to review and repeat the scripture out loud. You might even like to have an audio version of the verse that you can listen to. This can easily be done through apps on your phone. The most user friendly app I've found is The Bible App (https://www.bible.com/).

4. **Be creative.** Make your own **recording** of the verse on your device and listen to it over and over.

5. **Be committed.** While this might seem overwhelming on the front end, I promise that you will be blessed beyond your imagination as we work through this challenge.

I hope you will join me in this challenge and continue now to put God's word into your heart.

Blessings ...
Roy

WEEK ONE

"Let them give thanks to the LORD for his unfailing love and his wonderful deeds for mankind.
Psalm 107:8 NIV

Cicero wrote, "Gratitude is not only the greatest of virtues, but the parent of all the others."[1]

Gratitude is the bedrock of our disposition in life. Several years ago I was tasked with the responsibility of speaking to an influential group of business leaders about how to allow their faith to be a natural part of their business life. While flying back from Africa as I was praying, reading, and thinking about what I was going to say to them, the Lord impressed upon my heart three simple words. These three words nearly instantaneously became my mantra for many future lessons. It was on a United Airlines napkin that I scribbled down: grateful, gracious, and generous. Thus was born the "Three G's."

Whenever we begin (and end) our day in a place of gratitude, we will be stockpiling for the future. I encourage you to write down three things for which you are grateful each day and use them to remind yourself of all that God is doing in your life.

The Psalmist in this week's verse gives us three very specific things for which we should be grateful:

1. We are to be thankful **for the Lord**. We serve an awesome God who is supreme Lord over all. We have been given the wonderful privilege of not only having a God, but having a Lord. The word "Lord" here can be translated as, "the One who was, who is, and who always will be and the name in relation to God's redemptive work."

We serve a God who redeemed us and will never forsake us.

2. We are to be thankful **for all He is**. We will never be disappointed by the Lord. The Psalmist says, we are thankful for His unfailing love. The word literally means the Lord's mercy, goodness, faithfulness, love, and acts of kindness. The love of God is eternal. Paul wrote, *"For I am convinced that neither death, nor life, nor angels, nor principalities, nor things present, nor things to come, nor powers, nor height, nor depth, nor any other created thing, will be able to separate us from the love of God, which is in Christ Jesus our Lord"* (*Romans 8:38-39*).

3. We are to be thankful **for His wonderful deeds** for all mankind. The wonder of God is far above our comprehension. The Hebrew verb for "deed" means "to do something wonderful, to do something extraordinary, or difficult."[2] Although nothing is too hard or extraordinary for God, many of His deeds are beyond our abilities to comprehend. I think Isaiah says it best when he wrote, *"For My thoughts are not your thoughts, nor are your ways My ways,"* declares the LORD. *"For as the heavens are higher than the earth, so are My ways higher than your ways, and My thoughts than your thoughts."* (Isaiah 55:8–9)

I feel so strongly about how important it is to reflect on the Three G's that I have included them here at the end of every week. You will see a powerful change in yourself when you look on your life and consider what you are grateful for, where you can be more gracious, and how you will express generosity.

The Week in Review!

Write this week's verse:

Let them give thanks to the Lord for his unfailing love and His wonderful deeds for mankind. Psalm 107:8 NIV

The thing(s) I'm most **grateful** for this week:

1.

2.

3.

How will I be **GRACIOUS** to others because of this week?

How will I be **GENEROUS** next week?

WEEK TWO

"Trust in the Lord with all your heart and lean not on your own understanding."
Proverbs 3:5 NIV

I'm not much of a video game player. My grandsons, on the other hand, are. The oldest grandson got *Madden 16* for Christmas, and he has been teaching me to play it with him. The movement of the buttons and the toggles on the controller seem completely counterintuitive to me. I find myself being frustrated because I think I should understand how to play this child's game. Jayden keeps saying to me, "Just trust me, Pop-Pop, I'm telling you right!"

That reminds me of what this week's verse teaches. The key to everything is TRUST. All of us have our trust placed in some*one* or some*thing*. Maybe you trust your mind, your methods, or your money. Perhaps you lean on your abilities, attributes, and attitudes. It could be your health, wealth, or wisdom. In the end these will all fail us.

This line, from Proverbs 3, tells us clearly in whom we must place our trust. God is completely dependable. He is expressly divine. His character is so absolutely holy that it is impossible for Him to ever lie. His love is so pure that He can never do anything that is unkind, unjust, unfair, or unnecessary. He is the One we can TRUST.

The scripture doesn't stop there. It goes on to say that we must trust in Him with all our heart. Too often we have a divided heart. We want to compartmentalize our life. We think that it is okay to be one thing today and something different tomorrow. John Phillips reminded us that trusting God with anything less than "all our heart" is an insult to God. He wrote, "A divided heart and a double mind are almost as bad as no trust at all."[3]

This verse concludes with a warning about self-reliance: DON'T DO IT. Never lean on your own understanding. The more we put the Word of God into our hearts, minds, and life, the more we will understand how little understanding we have. Always remember our understanding comes as the result of our obedience. *"Trust in the Lord with all your heart and lean not on your own understanding."*

The Week in Review!

Write this week's verse:

Trust in the Lord with all your heart and lean not on your own understand: Proverbs 3:5

The thing(s) I'm most **grateful** for this week:

1.

2.

3.

How will I be **GRACIOUS** to others because of this week?

How will I be **GENEROUS** next week?

WEEK THREE

"Pray without ceasing."
1 Thessalonians 5:17 KJV

Most people find it difficult to actually talk anymore. Each day I am inundated with communications from people around the world, but more than 70% of this communication is not spoken. Too often we text rather than talk, email rather than engage, chat rather than converse, and post to Twitter or Instagram rather than participate in someone else's life. These efforts to connect with each other actually make us more disconnected with the person.

It is possible that our spiritual communication with God is equally shallow.

Paul says, *"pray without ceasing."* This is an exhortation and a command for believers which we must never neglect. Prayer should be an integrated component of the Christian's life.

In the midst of his letter to the Christians at Thessalonica Paul says *"pray without ceasing."* In this, the earliest canonical letter of Paul, the Apostle is reminding his readers that Jesus is coming again. Every chapter in this letter ends with a reference to the second coming of Jesus and with this in mind he writes, *"pray without ceasing."*

Read the entire context of this verse: *"Rejoice always; pray without ceasing; in everything give thanks; for this is God's will for you in Christ Jesus"* (5:16-18).

Paul is simply identifying what should be the proper and essential attitude of all believers. Jesus is coming again! In light of this fact we are called to rejoice. No matter what the world says, Jesus IS coming again! We can, and should, have joy in our hearts at all times, but this is impossible without the power of God reigning in our hearts, minds, and life.

When our hearts are filled with JOY, we will pray because we know that we are both insufficient and inefficient on our own. The New Testament word for prayer "encompasses all the aspects of prayer: submission, confession, petition, intercession, praise, and thanksgiving."[4]

Prayer is simply communicating with God. We talk to Him, we share our hearts with Him, and we listen to Him through His word. This year as you are memorizing scripture I trust you will realize that you are constantly hearing from God, therefore, *"Pray without ceasing."*

The Week in Review!

Write this week's verse:

The thing(s) I'm most *grateful* for this week:
1.

2.

3.

How will I be **GRACIOUS** to others because of this week?

How will I be **GENEROUS** next week?

WEEK FOUR

"Therefore, if anyone is in Christ, he is a new creation; the old has gone, the new has come!"
2 Corinthians 5:17 NIV

Once again this week we find something about the old and the new. In this fourth week of a new year I want you to remember: "That was then... THIS is now!"

The marvelous grace and mercy of God is sufficient to reach all who believe – from the best person to the worst, we are all are separated from God by sin. The good news is that God sent His son, His ONLY son, Jesus, into the world to be the sacrifice for our sins. The substitutionary death of Jesus on the cross (Jesus became your sin) and His glorious resurrection from the grave is the transformational power of grace.

God is not in the business of *reforming* us. Reformation is making something different from the same material. God is in the business of **transforming** us. He makes us a NEW creation!

If you know Jesus as your personal Lord and Savior, then you are NEW. What does that mean? The old values, plans, ideas, loves, desires, beliefs, practices, tendencies, loyalties, ambitions, drive, determination and the like are gone. Because Jesus is reigning in our lives, we want what He wants. We do what He does. We think like He thinks. We live like He lives.

This does not imply that we always get it right. We will fall back and drift away too often, but the abiding presence of Jesus in our lives draws us back into proper perspective as we are conformed to the image of Christ.

You do not have to live in the past. Jesus empowers us to be continually growing in His knowledge and grace. You are a NEW CREATION!

The Week in Review!

Write this week's verse:

The thing(s) I'm most *grateful* for this week:
1.

2.

3.

How will I be **GRACIOUS** to others because of this week?

How will I be **GENEROUS** next week?

WEEK FIVE

"Be on your guard; stand firm in the faith; be courageous; be strong."
1 Corinthians 16:13 NIV

Life is more of a battlefield than it is a playground. Matthew Henry wrote, "A Christian is always in danger, therefore should ever be on the watch. He should be fixed in the faith of the gospel, and never desert or give it up. By this faith alone he will be able to keep his ground in an hour of temptation. Christians should be careful that charity not only reigns in their hearts, but shines in their lives."[5]

As we navigate this thing we call life, Paul gives us four clear admonitions:

1. **Be on your guard** because we are never safe from attack. It is in those places in your life where you think you are safe that you are in the greatest danger. The writer of Proverbs said, *"Guard your heart above all else, for it determines the course of your life" (4:23).* We primarily guard our hearts and minds by pouring the Word of God into them. Hopefully this One-A-Week Challenge is encouraging you in this.

2. **Stand firm in the faith** simply means that we must have stability in our lives. We must have a strong foundation on which we build everything we do. If we are not grounded in "the faith" we will fall for anything. "The Faith" that Paul writes of here is not the faith of trusting but the faith of truth. In other words, he is talking about the content of the gospel. The truth of Jesus Christ. Too many people in Corinth were, as those in the world today, are swayed by everything under the sun. Our security is in the gospel of Jesus

Christ. He is not the best way to God, He is the
ONLY way to God.

3. **Be courageous.** A better translation of this
   portion of this verse reads, *"act like men!"* (1 Cor.
   16:13) He is imploring them to have the courage
   to stand up against the attacks, assaults, and
   accusations of the enemy.

4. **Be strong** concludes his admonitions. A
   constant reminder of Paul throughout his
   writings is the matter of being strong in the Lord
   (see Eph. 6:10-18). Another great reminder of
   this truth, and one of my favorites, is in Joshua
   1:6-9.

I trust that as we memorize this verse we will take heed
and materialize this verse in our hearts, minds, and
lives.

The Week in Review!

Write this week's verse:

The thing(s) I'm most *grateful* for this week:
1.

2.

3.

How will I be **GRACIOUS** to others because of this week?

How will I be **GENEROUS** next week?

WEEK SIX

"And whatever you do, do it heartily, as to the Lord and not to men."
Colossians 3:23 NKJV

Warren Wiersbe wrote that the principles of obedience apply to any kind of honest employment. A Christian worker ought to be the best worker on the job. He ought to obey orders and not argue. He ought to serve Christ and not the boss only, and he ought to work whether anybody is watching or not. If he follows these principles, he will receive his reward from Christ even if his earthly master (his boss) does not recognize him or reward him."[6]

Not everyone loves their job. Too many people see their employment as an obligation and a burden rather than an opportunity and a blessing. I am trying desperately to be a better listener so that I might be a better leader. What I hear most is complaining, much of which is centered around people and their jobs. Is there a way to move people from complaining to celebrating? Is it possible? Think about these three words:

Perspective changes everything. When we submit to the Lord with our heart, we understand that He is Lord of EVERYTHING. Most of our complaining about our circumstances is the result our own personal demands. When we realize that God is the boss of us and that everything we do is in His presence, we will certainly have a different perspective. Think about it this way. Every meeting you attend, every face-to-face conversation you have, every phone call you make, every customer or client with whom you engage is God's assignment for you at that moment. Ask yourself the questions, "Did my conversation honor God?" and "Did that person see the love of Jesus in me?" That's a new perspective!

Persistence is always necessary. Not everything goes the way you have planned. Life is simple, but not easy. We are often distracted and driven by every wind that blows. When we realize that we work for an "audience of One," we will have the power to persist amidst the trials. Jesus told his disciples, *"Whoever the Father gives to me I will certainly never cast them out"* John 6:37 (paraphrased). Even in the middle of the storms, be persistent, knowing that we are never alone.

Passion will cause others to be impacted and influenced. When we perform our responsibilities with passion, others will notice. Be passionate about your work. Put your absolute best into every aspect of your work life and your entire association will be impacted. Martin Luther King, Jr. said,

> If a man is called to be a street sweeper, he should sweep streets even as Michelangelo painted, or Beethoven composed music, or Shakespeare wrote poetry. He should sweep streets so well that all the hosts of heaven and earth will pause to say, here lived a great street sweeper who did his job well.[7]

Remember to do all that you do as unto the Lord!

The Week in Review!

Write this week's verse:

The thing(s) I'm most *grateful* for this week:
1.

2.

3.

How will I be **GRACIOUS** to others because of this week?

How will I be **GENEROUS** next week?

Week Seven

**"For where your treasure is,
there your heart will be also."**
Luke 12:34 NKJV

When the Bible speaks of the "heart," it refers to the center of our being. The word "occurs over one thousand times in the Bible, making it the most common anthropological term in the Scripture. It denotes a person's center for both physical and emotional-intellectual-moral [and spiritual] activities."[8]

This week's verse tells us that whatever we treasure in our life will be the controller of our life. Whatever is most precious will consume us. What do you treasure the most? Be honest. It could be money, power, fame, or anything else. Think about it another way. What is the directing force in your life? What are you pursuing? What motivates you to get up every day and do the things you do? What is the goal of your life?

While it is advisable and admirable to work diligently in your sphere of influence because, as we learned last week, we are working for the Lord and not for people, our chief aim in life must not simply be the pursuit of riches and fame. Jesus said that the greatest commandment is to *"Love the Lord your God with all your heart and with all your soul and with all your mind"* (Mt.22:37).

In other places Jesus talks about our heart's treasure chest.

> *Do not store up for yourselves **treasures on earth**, where moth and rust destroy, and where thieves break in and steal. But store up for yourselves **treasures in heaven**, where moth and rust do not destroy, and where thieves do not*

break in and steal. For where your treasure is, there your heart will be also" (Matt.6:19-21).

"For the mouth speaks out of that which fills [is treasured in] the heart" (Mt. 12:34b).

As you memorize this verse, think about what you are truly treasuring in your heart.

The Week in Review!

Write this week's verse:

The thing(s) I'm most *grateful* for this week:
1.

2.

3.

How will I be **GRACIOUS** to others because of this week?

How will I be **GENEROUS** next week?

WEEK EIGHT

"I can do all things through Christ who strengthens me."
Philippians 4:13 KJV

If you are a parent, you will remember teaching your children to tie their shoes. You worked and worked with them, but over and over you heard them say, "I can't do it!" In the early stages of the process, perhaps they did not possess the ability to finish the project, but as time progressed, it was not so much their lack of knowledge as their lack of desire. Also, they had gently learned that if they didn't tie their shoes you would do it for them. Eventually they learned the task and have since been tying their own shoes.

Saying "I can't" can be a dangerous position to take. It often means that we are unwilling to **surrender** to an authority, trust a process, or acknowledge a need.

The context of Paul's comment this week relates to his gratitude for a gift that the Church in Philippi had given to him for his ministry. He is quick to point out that he is not complaining about the lack of gifts, for he says,

> *How I praise the Lord that you are concerned about me again. I know you have always been concerned for me, but you didn't have the chance to help me. Not that I was ever in need, for I have learned how to be content with whatever I have. I know how to live on almost nothing or with everything. I have learned the secret of living in every situation, whether it is with a full stomach or empty, with plenty or little. For I can do everything through Christ,[a] who gives me strength. Even so, you have done well to share with me in my present difficulty"* (vv10-14).

Paul had learned the secret of contentment, and because of this, he was empowered with the assurance that "can't" was not a part of his vocabulary. He knew that no matter how hard the struggles in life could be, he had a sovereign foundation that assured him that "no matter what" God was his strength.

It is important to realize that when Paul said these words he was not talking about spiritual things, but rather physical things. He knew what God had done in him spiritually would translate to the physical. In other words, because of his spiritual union with Christ, he knew that whatever physical assignment was given to him (by Christ), he had the "I can do it" attitude because he would be strengthened to do it.

I hope we will stop thinking about the things we say "I can't" to and start saying, "because of Christ ... I CAN ... and ... I WILL!"

The Week in Review!

Write this week's verse:

The thing(s) I'm most *grateful* for this week:
1.

2.

3.

How will I be **GRACIOUS** to others because of this week?

How will I be **GENEROUS** next week?

WEEK NINE

"And My God shall supply all your need
according to His riches in glory by Christ Jesus."
Philippians 4:19 NKJV

Most of us struggle with control. One of the fundamental truths of life is this:

God is in control – I am not.

While He may assign certain aspects of life, over which I have "charge," I am never in control. I do not want to be in control, because I am not able to handle the pressure of holding it all together.

In last week's verse Paul boldly proclaimed that He could do all things through Christ and this week he explains further his faith in Christ. Paul has come to understand the mystery of the faith. Remember Paul is writing the Christians at Philippi a note of gratitude for the generous financial gift he has received from them. His gratitude was based in the great truth that he had learned from the Father. Pastor John MacArthur writes,

> Paul knew that the Philippians would not only receive spiritual blessings in heaven for their generosity, but also that **God** would **supply all** their physical **needs** in this life. The Philippians had sacrificially (cf. 2 Cor. 8:1-3) given of their earthly possessions to support God's servant, Paul. In return, God would amply supply their needs; He would not be in their debt. Having sown bountifully, they would reap bountifully (2 Cor. 9:6); having "honor[ed] the Lord from [their] wealth and from the first of all [their] produce... [their] barns will be filled with plenty and [their] vats will overflow with new wine" (Prov. 3:9-10).

They would discover that it is impossible to out-give God.[9]

Our attitude towards money is really an indicator about our attitude towards God. Many people have failed to acknowledge that God owns it all. As I have written previously,

I am a steward, not an owner of anything.

Every aspect of life is owned by God. He entrusts certain things into my care but I must always understand that it all belongs to God. I must faithfully discharge all that He has put in my care.

A faithful grasp of this truth causes me to trust Him fully. As the owner of everything, God has His name on the line. As our verses thus far this year have been teaching us, God has everything in His control. The Word has encouraged, commanded, instructed, and continues to teach us that He [God] can be fully trusted.

Why is it that we have such difficulty in trusting Him with money? Could it be that even though we say the words "it's all God's" we still believe that it is ours to share with Him? For what does God need money? What will God lack without your support? The bottom line truth is that God gives us this simple way of exhibiting our trust in Him. Why would we trust God with our soul and not trust Him with "our" money? Since we know that He is sufficient for eternity shouldn't we realize that He is sufficient for every day?

The very nature of Holy God is to be fully independent of anyone or anything else. All *"His riches in glory"* are available to all believers! He is the supply of everything you need, but we must also remember that He is the supplier of everything you have.

The Week in Review!

Write this week's verse:

The thing(s) I'm most *grateful* for this week:
1.

2.

3.

How will I be **GRACIOUS** to others because of this week?

How will I be **GENEROUS** next week?

WEEK TEN

"For I know the plans I have for you," declares the Lord. "Plans to prosper you and not to harm you, plans to give you hope and a future."
Jeremiah 29:11 NIV

What are you planning today? If you are like me, you spend some time each week or day planning what lies ahead. I get to my office each morning and glance at my day's agenda and then set out to accomplish all that is there. It usually works pretty well because I have learned (most time) to, as Margaret Thatcher is credited with saying, "Plan your work for today and every day, then work your plan."[10] We have all heard this in one form or another and have tried to implement this tactic.

There are only three probable places we find ourselves in life. I heard someone say, we are either drifting, driven, or directed. The truth is we all find ourselves in one or more of these places from time to time.

When one is **drifting,** he is influenced greatly by the circumstances. Picture a person floating in a tube on the lake on a calm day. As long as there is no wind or boats or anything else his drifting is very pleasurable. Now picture a storm building or a few boats speeding by this person and realize that everything about his situation is changing. Whichever way the wind blows or the waves push him he will go. This person is controlled by the circumstances!

A **driven** person fundamentally acts and believes he is completely in control. He drives himself wherever he wants. This person might be highly successful, but the truth of the matter is he can only drive so far. Most driven people find themselves driven in only one area of their life and it is usually in their professional life. They work hard and achieve a measure of success, but the time comes when they feel like they have earned the right to ease up a bit and this easing usually causes them to fall back into drifting.

A **directed** person is one who is intentionally aware that he is directed by someone larger than himself. In the purest sense he knows that God is in control and is directing him from the front. The director always leads from the front. The bible is replete with descriptions and examples of this style of God's leadership for our lives. Jesus said *"Follow Me"* no fewer than 14 times in the New Testament.

The verse this week clearly points out three things:

1. God knows the plans He has for us. This is God's plan. He is the architect of the plan. The plan has been fully developed and because of this, God is willing to declare it to you through His Word. (Psalm 1:6)

2. His plans are for His glory and our good. His plan will protect you and never harm you. Everywhere God directs us we can know that He is in front of us. He is both our protector and provision.

3. The plan of God is both for you now and in the future. The beauty of the Christian life is that we are never alone. He gives us hope in the day-to-day struggles and He reminds us of our future. He is in control.

When you find yourself adrift, remember God has a plan. When you are driving yourself, be careful and remember the only plan that works is the one you know certainly comes from God. Yes, He has a plan!

The Week in Review!

Write this week's verse:

The thing(s) I'm most *grateful* for this week:
1.

2.

3.

How will I be **GRACIOUS** to others because of this week?

How will I be **GENEROUS** next week?

WEEK ELEVEN

"You keep in perfect peace those whose minds are steadfast, because they trust in You!
Isaiah 26:3 NLT

The ideal of peace is something for which all humanity strives. In the face of global conflicts, battles, and wars, the world calls for peace, but none seems forthcoming. American Poet Henry Wadsworth Longfellow wrote, "And in despair I bowed my head; 'There is no peace on earth' I said; 'For hate is strong, and mocks the song of peace on earth, good-will to men!'"[11] This verse from a Christmas carol was based on the 1863 poem he wrote in the midst of the United States Civil War, but is appropriate to much more than that era.

Peace is illusive because it is in opposition to human nature. We live in a fallen world which is under the rule of Satan. Jesus referred to him as *"the ruler of this world"* (John 12:31), and Paul calls him *"the prince of the power of the air"* (Ephesians 2:2), and *"the god of this world"* (2 Corinthians 4:4). John makes a further distinction when he says: *"We know that we are of God, and the whole world is in the power of the evil one"* (1 John 5:19).

Remember, Satan is a liar and always lies. Nothing this world tells you is ultimately true. The world's system may contain some true things but it is not truth. Jesus said in John 17:17 that the Word of God is truth and from His Word comes peace.

God is the author of peace and He gives, keeps, and promises peace. Peace is not simply the absence of conflict, but the confidence in the midst of conflict. Peace is not an idea, it is a person. This week's verse promises that we will have peace as the result of our minds being firm and unwavering in our trust in God!

The Week in Review!

Write this week's verse:

The thing(s) I'm most *grateful* for this week:
1.

2.

3.

How will I be **GRACIOUS** to others because of this week?

How will I be **GENEROUS** next week?

WEEK TWELVE

"If any of you lacks wisdom, let him ask God, who gives generously to all without reproach, and it will be given to him."
James 1:5 ESV

Most of us do not want to viewed as "needy" and therefore we are afraid to ask for help. Often we mistakenly think that asking is a sign of weakness. In reality the willingness to ask is a sign of strength. The proud believe in self-sufficiency, but this is the highest pinnacle of foolish vanity.

Life is a series of tests and at times these can sometimes be frustrating. My friend Jimmy Draper is known for saying, "Christianity is not a way of doing certain things, it is a certain way of doing everything." How do we know how to live in this certain way?

James points out in this verse three things the believer must understand.

1. We all **need** wisdom. When the challenges of life come upon us, we must understand that we lack of knowing what to do. Wisdom is more than knowledge or information. Wisdom is applying faith to the circumstances of life. It is living like Jesus lived – in step with God's will.

2. We should **ask** for wisdom. The very nature of God is generosity and as this verse states, He generously gives without reproach. The word "ask" translated specifically means the act of "asking for God to give us something." It is not simply asking God to do something for us; it implies our desperation before God. We have the unique opportunity to ask our Heavenly Father for something that only He can give.

3. We can **receive** wisdom. James writes here, "it will be given to him." Our Father does not rebuke us for not having wisdom. Without a hint of scolding, He offers us a full supply of wisdom. John Phillips wrote,

> Much of the wisdom that we need, and for which we pray, is to be found in His Word. It is already ours, available to us in hundreds of precepts, proverbs, parables, and principles. Solomon wrote a whole book of proverbs, pithy sayings full of the distilled wisdom of heaven for life on earth. The parables of the Lord Jesus are gems of wisdom. The great principles unfolded in both the Sermon on the Mount and the Epistles are sublime. The Bible is full of wise counsel. It speaks authoritatively to all aspects of human life. It speaks clearly. It makes no mistakes. It is infallible and unerring in its judgments. All we have to do is read it, study it, meditate upon it, memorize it, and obey it.[12]

The Week in Review!

Write this week's verse:

The thing(s) I'm most *grateful* for this week:
1.

2.

3.

How will I be **GRACIOUS** to others because of this week?

How will I be **GENEROUS** next week?

WEEK THIRTEEN

"Your word is a lamp for my feet, [and] a light on my path"
Psalm 119:105 NIV

On any journey, it is important to know where we are going. Perhaps you spent time setting goals this year, and if so, you probably have a path to meet those goals. It is always easier to stay on the intended path when there is light on the path.

A few years ago in West Africa I remember one evening vividly. Two of us were making our way back to our hotel from our final speaking assignment that day. The night sky was so dark and the roads were so bad that we were moving along in the vehicle at a snail's pace.

We came to a fork in the road and our driver told us that he wanted us to get out of the truck and walk straight up the road because he had to drop off some of our local pastors in a nearby village.

He said, "the path to the village is very difficult and dangerous for travel. I want you to walk along and I will meet you at the crossroad ahead."

Thankful for his concern for us, we got out of the truck and began to walk along the road. With the tail lights from the vehicle now gone we suddenly realized just how dark it was.

Armed with only a flashlight, we walked along. I remember shining the light down at my feet to be sure of the next step and them shining it up the road to make sure our direction was steady. That encounter forever cemented this verse of scripture into my heart!

The word of God will give you clarity for each step you take but it will also keep your path illuminated.

Jesus is the Light of the World and His word is all that you need to keep moving in the right direction. (By the way, the driver did meet us at the crossroad!)

The Week in Review!

Write this week's verse:

The thing(s) I'm most *grateful* for this week:
1.

2.

3.

How will I be **GRACIOUS** to others because of this week?

How will I be **GENEROUS** next week?

WEEK FOURTEEN

"For he satisfies the thirsty and fills the hungry with good things."
Psalm 107:9 NIV

In 1965 The Rolling Stones released the song "(I Can't Get No) Satisfaction." The song was about the vain attempts of finding satisfaction in the material world.

True satisfaction in this regard is illusory. The problem is that most people view satisfaction as something that we can achieve. This erroneous idea places the emphasis on ourselves and our abilities. The world calls out to us with a plethora of things that it promises will bring satisfaction. These are empty promises.

By contrast, the Word of God calls out to us with spiritual principles that tell us that satisfaction is not something we achieve but rather something we receive. This is the Christian perspective, namely, that the blessings of God are dependent upon Him and not man. A personal relationship with God through the Lord Jesus is vital to our ultimate satisfaction.

The human heart is dry, parched, and athirst. We are in need of quenching waters that will satisfy. Only God can provide this. The Psalmist says that a man who takes in the Word of God with delight and meditates on it day and night *"will be like a tree planted by the rivers of water"* (Psalm 1:3), thereby bringing forth fruit and satisfaction.

The soul of man is desperately starved with a vacuous hole needing to be filled. Nothing on earth can satisfy this void. God alone is our supply and our sustenance and therefore our satisfaction. Jesus said, *"I am the bread of life; he who comes to Me will not hunger"*

(John 6:35a). This satisfaction came down from the Heavenly Father in the person of Christ.

Although the world cries out that it will meet our needs, scratch our itch, and fill our lives, it does so only temporarily and superficially. Our verse today from the Word of God sings the song about God satisfying and filling! Look to Him today and be satisfied.

The Week in Review!

Write this week's verse:

The thing(s) I'm most *grateful* for this week:
1.

2.

3.

How will I be **GRACIOUS** to others because of this week?

How will I be **GENEROUS** next week?

WEEK FIFTEEN

"Do not be deceived: God cannot be mocked.
A man reaps what he sows."
Galatians 6:7 NIV

When Paul says, *"God cannot be mocked,"* he uses a word that means "to turn up your nose at." Few of us would readily admit that we have turned our nose up to God, but whenever we choose to reject His word, that is exactly what we are doing.

We are 15 weeks into our "One-A-Week Challenge" where we have been attempting to memorize a verse of scripture a week. At the outset this seemed daunting, but as time has marched on I hope you have found, as I have found from others who have taken this challenge in the past, that this journey has been encouraging and exciting for you.

Each week we are looking at the Word of God. Every word of God is completely true and trustworthy. The surest way to know the God of the Word is to know the Word of God. Not everything that we hear from the world is true. There are now, as there have always been, false and satanic teachers who impose their views in juxtaposition to God's truth. I hope you remember that truth is <u>not</u> a *position*...truth is a *person*. Jesus boldly proclaimed *"I am the way, the truth, and the life"* (John 14:6a). Elsewhere Jesus prayed, *"Sanctify them in the truth; Thy word is truth"* (John 17:17). The exact opposite of truth is deception, which is a lie. Remember, Satan is the father of lies. Although he has no power to defeat God, he is skilled at lying and convincing the weak that the lie is preferable to truth.

One of the salient truths of life is summed up thusly: "Whatever is in the well, comes up in the bucket." Our life becomes a living testimony to whatever we pour or sow into our lives. One English writer observed, "What strikes me more and more each day is the permanence of one's early life, the identity between youth and manhood. Every habit, good and bad, of those early years seems to have permanently affected my whole life. The battle is largely won or lost before it seems to begin."[13]

This proclamation of Paul from Galatians is one of the divine laws of scripture. Even the redeemed are not immune from this law. While it is true that we will never reap the full consequences of our sin, we can still reap the heartaches, headaches, wounds, and shame of our actions. Remember, when God convicts you of your sin, you are being reminded by the Holy Spirit that you no longer have to continue in those ways. Receive the rebuke as an opportunity for repentance.

The bible nowhere teaches that we can be sinless, but it does tell us that we can sin LESS. Be careful what you sow. Live in the Light of God's word and sow those things into your life that are a reflection of Jesus Christ.

The Week in Review!

Write this week's verse:

The thing(s) I'm most *grateful* for this week:
1.

2.

3.

How will I be **GRACIOUS** to others because of this week?

How will I be **GENEROUS** next week?

WEEK SIXTEEN

"The LORD is my shepherd; I shall not want."
Psalm 23:1 ESV

This is one of the most beloved passages in all of scripture. No one knows exactly when David penned these words. Some believe he wrote it as an old man approaching physical death and that this is a hymn of reflection over his full life. Others think it came in his youth. Either way, imagine the shepherd boy sitting under the shade of a huge tree, watching his flock feast on the pasture around him or drinking from a babbling brook meandering through the meadow.

David begins by saying *"The LORD"*, using one of the primary and regular words for Jehovah in the Old Testament. The name identifies God as the One who is, who was, and who will be. In other words, He is the eternal One. This is the One, the Word made flesh – Jesus.

The sentence continues, *"The LORD is **MY** shepherd."* The idea here is not of a mere shepherd. He did not even say he was THE shepherd, although He is. David says, He is My shepherd. David is singing out that he has a personal and powerful relationship with HIS shepherd and because of this relationship, he would never want for anything.

The fact that God makes available for us the possibility of a genuine personal relationship with Him is incredible. No religion on earth makes this claim. He has not given us a set of rules to follow, a dogma to live by, or a moral code to meet. Jesus has not said, "be better ... get good ...try harder ... study more" ... or any such thing. The crux of knowing Him is by grace through faith. A personal relationship with Christ is the result of His redeeming work on the cross. Paul said, *"But God demonstrates His own love toward us, in that while we were yet sinners, Christ died for us"* (Romans 5:8).

Read in context from a modern translation this passage from Romans which brightly clarifies the love of God toward us.

> *Christ arrives right on time to make this happen. He didn't, and doesn't, wait for us to get ready. He presented himself for this sacrificial death when we were far too weak and rebellious to do anything to get ourselves ready. And even if we hadn't been so weak, we wouldn't have known what to do anyway. We can understand someone dying for a person worth dying for, and we can understand how someone good and noble could inspire us to selfless sacrifice. But God put his love on the line for us by offering his Son in sacrificial death while we were of no use whatever to him. Now that we are set right with God by means of this sacrificial death, the consummate blood sacrifice, there is no longer a question of being at odds with God in any way. If, when we were at our worst, we were put on friendly terms with God by the sacrificial death of his Son, now that we're at our best, just think of how our lives will expand and deepen by means of his resurrection life! Now that we have actually received this amazing friendship with God, we are no longer content to simply say it in plodding prose. We sing and shout our praises to God through Jesus, the Messiah!* (Romans 5:7-11 MSG)

It is only through acceptance of this great love that we are able, like David, to say, *"The Lord is MY shepherd."*

The Week in Review!

Write this week's verse:

The thing(s) I'm most *grateful* for this week:
1.

2.

3.

How will I be **GRACIOUS** to others because of this week?

How will I be **GENEROUS** next week?

WEEK SEVENTEEN

"Surely goodness and mercy shall follow me all the days of my life and I shall dwell in the house of the Lord forever."
Psalm 23:6 ESV

This week our verse comes as the closing refrain from last week's hymn. What began with David singing, "The Lord is My shepherd" ends with, *"I shall dwell in the house of the Lord forever."* The eternal home of every true believer is heaven, but the life of redeemed faith is not only for the future, it is for the present.

A more appropriate rendering of the word "surely" is "only" which implies that David knows exactly what is in front of him. Although David's life certainly was riddled with trials, temptations, and tempests, his future was sure because of the abiding presence of the Shepherd he called Lord. No matter the difficulties or dilemmas, his faith was sure – he would dwell in the house of the Lord forever.

"Charles Spurgeon, that famous preacher from London, used to call 'goodness and mercy' God's footmen. In his day, when a wealthy man traveled, two footmen took their place behind him on his coach. Their task was to smooth the way for him. Where he went, they went, always there. When his coach stopped, they jumped down to open the door for him. They would hurry into the inn to make sure his room was ready and his supper was served. God's two footmen are goodness and mercy and they follow us just like those footmen to smooth our journey home."[14]

Every moment we live between redemption and eternity is under the care and provision of God's goodness and mercy, but what does this mean?

David is confident that God can be trusted. One of the attributes of God is His goodness:

> *Oh, give thanks to the LORD, for He is good!*
> *For His mercy endures forever.*
> Psalm 107:1 NKJV

> *Oh, how great is Your goodness*
> Psalm 31:19 NKJV

From the opening chapters of the Bible we learn this fact. God proclaimed everything which He created *"good"* (see Gen. 1:4, 10, 18). His goodness is seen in every aspect of creation, thus we can, with certainty, join David in making this proclamation and because of this truth we can rest confident that we can trust God with all that we are.

The Week in Review!

Write this week's verse:

The thing(s) I'm most *grateful* for this week:
1.

2.

3.

How will I be **GRACIOUS** to others because of this week?

How will I be **GENEROUS** next week?

WEEK EIGHTEEN

"And we know that God causes all things to work together for good to those who love God, to those who are called according to His purpose."
Romans 8:28 NASB

Last week we learned that God's nature is goodness. This week we read that He causes all things to work together for good. Seems logical right? Why then do we notice so many things that seem to be going in the wrong direction?

Most often the problem is with perspective. We imagine that God's purpose is for us to be on a smooth path free of turmoil. God's perfect peace is not the absence of conflict, it is rather an absolute awareness of His presence.

Scripture is replete in telling us that one of the attributes of God is His goodness. *"God saw all that He had made, and behold it was very good"* (Gen. 1:31). Since the very nature of God is goodness, we must remember that we are not tasked with earning this goodness, rather we can experience it by grace through faith. God's goodness is shown even to the unrighteous and unbelieving. The Psalmist wrote: *"The Lord is good to all, and his mercy is over all that he has made"* (Psalm 145:9). This being noted, we must acknowledge another truth.

When things seem out of control we must remember one of the fundamental truths of life:

"God is in control – I am not."

While He may assign to me certain aspects of life over which I have "charge," I am never in control. I do not want to be in control, because I am not able to handle the pressure of holding it all together. This is the central truth of Paul's affirmation in today's verse. He is proclaiming,

> "And we know with an absolute knowledge that for those who are loving God, all things are working together resulting in good, for those who are divinely summoned according to His purposes" [paraphrase] because of his absolute trust in God.

The fact that God is in control is irrefutable, undeniable, and absolute. Psalm 33 is a great reminder of this fact. His control is independent of our trust or faith. He is in control. God is the divine cause of all things and because of His nature of complete goodness, we know that His purposes will be worked out in our lives day by day. Although we may not completely see the goodness in all that takes place around us, our faith IN God and our knowledge OF God assures us that He can be fully trusted.

The Week in Review!

Write this week's verse:

The thing(s) I'm most *grateful* for this week:
1.

2.

3.

How will I be **GRACIOUS** to others because of this week?

How will I be **GENEROUS** next week?

WEEK NINETEEN

"If God is for us, who can be against us?"
Romans 8:31b ESV

The greatest security in all of creation is summed up in this verse of scripture. In the midst of this magnificent chapter of the Bible is contained, what John MacArthur calls, "a hymn of security." It must be remembered that these verses are written to true Christians who have become identified with Christ through saving faith offered by Him to all who truly believe.

The verse begins with the word "if." This does not imply a possibility, but a certainty. The better translation of this would read, *"**Because** God is for us, who can be against us?"* The scope of this verse of scripture is within the context of our being eternally saved by the grace and goodness of God in Christ Jesus.

Many things clamor to take away from us what God has given us. In the New Testament era the Jewish community proclaimed to Christians the necessity of keeping the ritual laws of the Mosaic covenant (see Acts 15:1-29). Even today the Roman Catholic Church teaches that one might lose their salvation by committing "mortal sins" (although it claims the power for itself the ability to give and take grace), a doctrine that has absolutely no foundation in scripture.

With regard to salvation remember this:

> If we can be bad enough to lose it,
> We had to be good enough to get it!

Jesus' sacrificial death on the cross is both the foundation and security of our salvation. When we are saved, we are secure, and we can be sure. If you ever have pause to think that the enemies of God are too big, remember what Isaiah wrote:

> *Surely our griefs He Himself [Christ, the Son] bore, and our sorrows He carried; yet we ourselves esteemed Him stricken, smitten of God [the Father], and afflicted. But He was pierced through for our transgressions, He was crushed for our iniquities; the chastening for our well-being fell upon Him, and by His scourging we are healed. All of us like sheep have gone astray, each of us has turned to his own way; but the Lord has caused the iniquity of us all to fall on Him.... But the Lord [the Father] was pleased to crush Him [the Son], putting Him to grief; if He would render Himself as a guilt offering (Isaiah. 53:4-6,10).*

Do you have this assurance?

The Week in Review!

Write this week's verse:

The thing(s) I'm most *grateful* for this week:
1.

2.

3.

How will I be **GRACIOUS** to others because of this week?

How will I be **GENEROUS** next week?

WEEK TWENTY

"In everything give thanks; for this is God's will for you in Christ Jesus."
1 Thessalonians 5:18 NASB

For much of my life I have been talking about the three "G's" of living. Grateful, generous, and gracious are three words that should summarize the living out of our faith in a personal and tangible way.

Being **grateful** is the very essence of the redeemed. Everything we have in life is a gift from God. From that initial gasp for air that draws breath into a newborn's lungs to the final exhale from an aged body and everything in between is because of the good hand of our Heavenly Father. God's provision for us is far beyond words on a page. God has so perfectly provided for everything. It is spiritually abnormal for Christians to be unthankful.

John MacArthur wrote,

> Unthankfulness disobeys the many Scripture texts that enjoin the believer to a life of gratitude. Romans 8:28 sets forth the overarching principle: "And we know that God causes all things to work together for good to those who love God, to those who are called according to His purpose." God's providence—His sovereign blending of all of life's contingencies for believers' ultimate blessing—causes them to be thankful for everything in life, knowing that it fits into His eternal purpose for them (cf. Genesis 50:20; Psalms 37:28; 91:3-4; 145:9 Proverbs 19:21).[15]

Too often we are only thankful for things. Paul, while not excluding this idea, is stating a far higher view of gratitude. He says, *"In everything give thanks..."*

which refers to all that occurs in life. In the midst of the struggles, difficulties, and bumps of life we are exhorted to "give thanks." This is certainly not something that comes naturally but is a gracious and generous expression of the Holy Spirit living in our life.

Perhaps today you are plagued by something very difficult. I do not pretend to know all that you are going through but I am certain that God's grace is sufficient for you. There is no mountain so high, no vallcy so deep, and no pain so great that God's love cannot overcome. In the middle of the storm, by God's grace, we can give thanks that He is with us right now and forever.

Paul finishes this week's verse by reminding us of the power that enables us to accomplish this part of God's will. Remember, it is the will of God that we give thanks in everything, and this is possible through a personal relationship with Jesus Christ. If you are lacking gratitude, perhaps you are lacking Jesus.

The Week in Review!

Write this week's verse:

The thing(s) I'm most *grateful* for this week:
1.

2.

3.

How will I be **GRACIOUS** to others because of this week?

How will I be **GENEROUS** next week?

WEEK TWENTY-ONE

**"God has not given us a spirit of fear,
but of power and of love and of a sound mind."**
2 Timothy 1:7 NKJV

In 1933, shortly after becoming President of the United States, Franklin Delano Roosevelt boldly declared, **"We have nothing to fear but fear itself!"**

He was wrong. As long as there are snakes, we have something else to fear as far as I'm concerned!

Do you know the name Eppie Lederer? I bet you do when I refer to her by her pen name, Ann Landers. The late columnist, who wrote for 47 years, purportedly received over 10,000 letters each week. She said that the single greatest theme of the correspondence dealt with the subject of fear.

Fear comes from the Greek word *phobia*. The dictionary lists over 700 different phobias. Acrophobia is the fear of high places. Claustrophobia is the fear of tight, closed places. Agoraphobia is the fear of crowds or open places. Ergophobia is the fear of work. My favorite, phobophobia is the fear of fear itself!

Of what are you afraid? Maybe it is the dentist... the doctor... the nurse? I watched a news show one night about a man who was afraid of dust. On this same show was a man who was afraid of clutter (in his house.)

Even followers of Jesus Christ have fears. People fear losing their health, their wealth, their friends, their families, or their fame. Second Timothy has an antidote for fear:

> *For God has not given us a spirit of fear, but of power and of love and of a sound mind. Therefore,*

*do not be ashamed of the testimony of our Lord,
nor of me, His prisoner, but share with me in the
sufferings for the gospel according to the power of
God, who has saved us and called us with a holy
calling, not according to our works, but according
to His own purpose and grace which was given to
us in Christ Jesus before time began.*
2 Tim 1:7-9 NKJV

All our earthly fears are overcome in the believer's life
by the power of God in that our assurance of eternal
security is guaranteed. God's nature is that of
generosity and graciousness which enables us to
respond in gratitude. He gives us His power, His love,
and His mind. Read this verse from another translation:

*For God has not given us a spirit of cowardice,
but of power, and of love, and of wise discretion.
Be not therefore ashamed of the testimony of our
Lord, nor of me his prisoner; but suffer evil along
with the glad tidings, according to the power of
God; who has saved us, and has called us with
a holy calling, not according to our works, but
according to [his] own purpose and grace, which
[was] given to us in Christ Jesus before [the] ages
of time.*[16]

The saint of God, yielded to the Spirit of God, should
never have his life characterized by fear.

The Week in Review!

Write this week's verse:

The thing(s) I'm most *grateful* for this week:
1.

2.

3.

How will I be **GRACIOUS** to others because of this week?

How will I be **GENEROUS** next week?

WEEK TWENTY-TWO

"For all have sinned and fall short of the glory of God."
Romans 3:23 NIV

Sin is becoming an archaic word. In our modern society we have replaced the word with more palatable ones like, mistake, error, or shortcoming. None of these do justice to the original Greek word, *hamartánō*. This word literally means, *"to miss a mark on the way, not to hit the mark, or one who keeps missing the mark in his relationship to God."* [17]

This week we begin to look at the three steps to heaven.

STEP ONE: We must face the TRUTH about OURSELVES.
We are all sinners! Remember what the Bible says: *"There is none righteous, not even one"* (Romans 3:10) *"for all have sinned and fall short of the glory of God"* (Romans 3:23) *"For the wages of sin is death, but the free gift of God is eternal life in Christ Jesus our Lord"* (Romans 6:23).

Perhaps it is important that we are reminded of **what sin is**. It is lying, stealing, cheating, having bad thoughts, saying and doing bad things. We all do these things but why? **Where did sin come from?**

When God created the world, He created one man and one woman and placed them in a place called Eden. The Bible tells us that Eden was a perfect place. There was no sickness, death, old age, trouble or problems. God gave the man and the woman everything they needed in the garden and they only had one rule to obey. God told them that they must not eat of the Tree of the Knowledge of Good and Evil. Of all the other trees in the garden they could eat freely, but they must not eat of this tree. The place was paradise, but they willingly chose to <u>disobey</u> God and because of their <u>sin</u>, they were banished from the garden and the curse of death was on them and their children.

Since the fall of humanity in the garden, every human being has been born with a sinful nature and thus separated from God. This means when we were born we were all born with a dirty heart. **It's not our <u>fault</u>, but it's our <u>problem</u>!**

It is our problem because the Bible says that no one with a dirty heart can come into God's clean heaven. *Nothing impure will ever enter it [heaven], nor will anyone who does what is shameful or deceitful, but only those whose names are written in the Lamb's book of life* (Revelations 21:26-27 NIV).

So there's **the problem**. We want to go to heaven and God wants us to come to heaven, but we are born with a **problem** that will keep us from going to heaven. Facing the truth of the human condition is the first step of entering into a right relationship with God. Our sin does not cause God to hate us, rather, the truth of God is expressed in this verse, "*But God demonstrates His own love toward us, in that while we were yet sinners, Christ died for us*" (Romans 5:8).

The Week in Review!

Write this week's verse:

The thing(s) I'm most *grateful* for this week:
1.

2.

3.

How will I be **GRACIOUS** to others because of this week?

How will I be **GENEROUS** next week?

WEEK TWENTY-THREE

"I am the way, and the truth, and the life. No one comes to the Father but through me."
John 14:6 NASB

The line in the sand between all religions is this authoritative claim by Jesus. Many people will proclaim that Jesus was a good teacher and a capable moral leader, but nothing more. While these first two claims are true, they are meaningless if He is not more.

The Bible tells us that Heaven is a prepared place for a prepared person. Heaven is not the reward of good or sincere people. It is the home of prepared people. Jesus said,

> *Let not your heart be troubled; believe in God, believe also in Me. In My Father's house are many dwelling places; if it were not so, I would have told you; for I go to prepare a place for you. And if I go and prepare a place for you, I will come again, and receive you to Myself; that where I am, there you may be also. And you know the way where I am going"* (John 14:1-4 NASB).

Jesus promised to prepare a place for us and He did. Heaven is this prepared place. He assures us that we can have a home in this place for all eternity, but we must take the necessary steps to be prepared. Last week our verse of scripture reminded us of the truth about ourselves: We are all sinners. This week's verse affirms the truth about Jesus.

STEP TWO: We must face the TRUTH about JESUS.
Jesus is God's only solution to our sin problem. But why does Jesus have to be the ONLY solution to our problem? Throughout the whole Bible, God says that without the shedding of pure innocent blood, we cannot

be forgiven or cleansed of our sins. In other words, someone or something that is pure and clean has to die and take the place of the sinner.

And according to the Law, one may almost say,
all things are cleansed with blood, and without
shedding of blood there is no forgiveness
(Hebrews 9:22 NASB)

In the <u>Old Testament</u> God said that the sinner could take a clean animal without spot or blemish to the temple and it could be offered in the place of the guilty sinner. The priest would shed the blood of the animal on the altar and when God saw the blood, the sinner could be forgiven and have his sin covered. The Old Testament sacrifices covered the sin but never cleansed the sin. Only Jesus can do this. But first, the innocent had to die for the guilty.

But now, in the New Testament, after 2,000 years, God said that he would not accept any more sacrifices of bulls, goats and lambs. He said that He would provide one final sacrifice for all the sins of the world that would ever be committed. So He sent His final sacrifice, and just like the Old Testament sacrifices that had to perfect and clean, this one did too! But this time the sacrifice would be a man: JESUS!

In the beginning was the Word and the Word was with
God, and the Word was God ... In Him was life, and
the life was the Light of men ... And the Word became
flesh and dwelt among us, and we saw His glory, glory
as of the only begotten from the Father, full of grace
and truth. (John 1: 1, 4,14 NASB)

Behold the Lamb of God who takes away the sin of the
world. (John 1: 29 NASB)

You know that He appeared in order to take away
sins; and in Him there is no sin.
(I John 3:5 NASB)

Jesus was born without sin and the Bible says that he lived for 33 years and never sinned, and then he was arrested and put on the cross. When they put the nails in his hands and feet and the spear into his side, the pure clean blood of the perfect sacrifice flowed down the cross and when God saw the blood of his son, he declared the price paid for all the sins of the world.

For God so loved the world, that He gave His only
begotten Son, and whoever believes in Him shall not
perish, but have eternal life.
(John 3:16 NASB)

He made Him who knew no sin to be sin on our
behalf, so that we might become the righteousness
of God in Him.
(2 Cor. 5:21 NASB)

He became God's solution to our problem. But the story doesn't end there. The Bible says that on the third day after His crucifixion, Jesus arose from the grave and just as He was victorious over the grave, when we die, we have the promise that we can be too.

The first step to heaven is to realize that we have a **problem**. We are all sinners with a dirty heart. The second step says God has provided the **solution** for us in Jesus.

The Week in Review!

Write this week's verse:

The thing(s) I'm most *grateful* for this week:
1.

2.

3.

How will I be **GRACIOUS** to others because of this week?

How will I be **GENEROUS** next week?

WEEK TWENTY-FOUR

**"For by grace you have been saved through faith;
and that not of yourselves, it is the gift of God."**
Ephesians 2:8 NASB

This is the third straight week that we have been reading and memorizing scripture that teaches us the three steps to heaven. Thus far we have learned Step One: The truth about ourselves – We are all sinners, which is our problem. Step Two: The truth about Jesus Christ – he is the provision and solution for our problem. This week we consider ...

STEP THREE: We must face the TRUTH about Eternity.

After this life is over, we are going to spend eternity in one of two places. It will either be in hell or in heaven – but we have a choice. We had no choice about where we were born, but we do have a choice about where we will spend eternity.

Remember, our sinful nature condemns us already. None of our good works, religious practices or anything else makes us fit for heaven, but Jesus alone did redeem us by His blood on the cross. But the question remains, "How do I know for sure that God has forgiven me of my sins and that I will go to heaven when I die?"

The Bible says,

*If we confess our sins, He is faithful and righteous to
forgive us ... and to cleanse us from all
unrighteousness.*
(I John 1:9 NASB)

*If you confess with your mouth Jesus as Lord, and
believe in your heart that God raised Him from the
dead, you shall be saved; for with the heart man
believes, resulting in righteousness, and with the
mouth he confesses, resulting in salvation.
For the Scripture says, "Whoever believes in Him
will not be disappointed."*
(Romans 10:9-11 NASB)

So how can a person have God's forgiveness, heaven
and eternal life, and Jesus as personal Savior and
Lord? By trusting in Christ and asking Him for
forgiveness. Take the step of faith described by another
meaning of FAITH: **F**orsaking **A**ll, **I T**rust **H**im.

You do this through a simple prayer reflecting your
desire for Christ to change your life. You don't need
fancy words – only an honest heart. You can pray
something like this:

Lord Jesus,
*I know I am a sinner and have displeased You in many
ways. I believe You died for my sin, and only through
faith in Your death and resurrection can I be forgiven. I
want to turn from my sin and ask You to come into my
life as my Savior and Lord. From this day on, I will follow
You by living a life that pleases You. Thank you, Lord
Jesus, for saving me. Amen.*

Accepting Christ is just the beginning of a wonderful
adventure with God! Get to know Him better in a
number of ways:
- Follow Christ's example in baptism.
- Join a church where you can worship God and
  grow in your faith.
- In your church, get involved in Sunday School
  and Bible study.

- Begin a daily personal worship experience with God where you study the Bible and pray.

Our friends, this is our hope for you! If you have never truly asked Jesus into your heart, we hope that you will do this today.

The Week in Review!

Write this week's verse:

The thing(s) I'm most *grateful* for this week:
1.

2.

3.

How will I be **GRACIOUS** to others because of this week?

How will I be **GENEROUS** next week?

WEEK TWENTY-FIVE

"I praise you because I am fearfully and wonderfully made; your works are wonderful, I know that full well."
Psalm 139:14 NIV

There is something supernatural and spectacular about the birth of a baby. We see in that precious little one something that is so far above our own imagination. It grieves me when I hear someone say that life begins at delivery rather than conception. One look at an ultrasound proves that unborn baby is much more than a blob of tissue.

Far beyond the ultrasound we can hold on to the Word of God. The Psalmist here proclaims what he knows – that I am "fearfully and wonderfully made." Warren Wiersbe wrote, "God formed us as He wants us to be, and we must accept His will no matter how we feel about our genetic structure, our look, or our abilities."[18]

In the preceding verse the Psalmist wrote that God "knit me together in my mother's womb." The meaning of that word is that he intricately embroidered me together. Think about it in these terms. The Lord weaves and embroiders a human being together in the mother's womb, yet human societies have opted for abortions which reject this miracle of God.

Regardless of the mores of a fallen society, we can join with the Psalmist in proclaiming that all the works of God are wonderful. While much of the world proclaims that there is no God, His Word boldly and repeatedly proclaims that He cannot be ignored.

Read the words of John Phillips: "If David knew enough to be awed, what about us? We know that every living creature is made up of microscopic cells so small that the letter O on this page would contain between thirty to forty thousand of them. Each microscopic cell is a world in itself, containing an estimated two hundred trillion tiny molecules of atoms. Each cell, in other words, is a micro-universe of almost unbelievable complexity. All these cells put together make up a living creature. Each cell has its own specialized function and each works to an intricate time table which tells it when to grow, when to divide, when to make hormones, when to die.

Every minute of every day, some three billion cells in the body die and the same number are created to take their place. During any given moment in the life of any one of these cells, thousands of events are taking place, each one being precisely coordinated at the molecular level by countless triggers. The human body has more than a million million of them—a million in each square inch of skin, thirty billion in the brain, billions of red blood cells in the veins. Obviously, such a complicated and unerring development of cells cannot possibly be the result of chance. "He created me!" David exclaimed."[19]

If today you are struggling with the concept of a loving, personal, and involved God, just look at the crown of His creative beings and consider the magnitude and majesty of a newborn baby and praise God for His blessings.

The Week in Review!

Write this week's verse:

The thing(s) I'm most *grateful* for this week:
1.

2.

3.

How will I be **GRACIOUS** to others because of this week?

How will I be **GENEROUS** next week?

WEEK TWENTY-SIX

"Love the LORD your God with all your heart and all your soul, and with all your strength."
Deuteronomy 6:5 NIV

One of the most interesting places I have ever visited is India. With all that is difficult about the place, the greatest conflict occurs within the religious environment of the country. While this nation is extremely religious, with more than 79.8% of them identified as Hindus, there is an absence of absolutes in nearly the total population. As I have shared the Gospel of Jesus Christ with thousands and thousands of Hindus, I have witnessed many of them take the decision to call on Jesus with "faith" only to watch them have a change of mind when I proclaim that Jesus ALONE is God, and all others are merely the works of man. In other words, they are eager to add Jesus to their list, but are unwilling to proclaim Him as the only Lord.

In Scripture the highest truth of God is that He alone is God. In Deuteronomy 6:4-9 we read "The Shema" which is the central prayer in the Jewish prayer book and is often the first section of Scripture that a Jewish child learns. Verse 4 declares, **"The LORD is one!"** There is none other than Him.

As the only true God, He gives us the right and responsibility to love Him. Our love for the LORD must be sincere and strong, which means that we do not simply love Him for **what He does**, but we love Him **for who He is**. As we think about this, we realize that we are nothing if not for Him. The love we have from Him comes from our heart, which is the seat of our understanding and the center of our personality. It is the inner nature of man, including his intellectual, emotional, and cognitive abilities. God is calling for us to be all in with our love for Him.

In a world that is constantly clamoring for our affection and attention, our Heavenly Father gives us a clear directive to set our heart and soul upon Him, above all else.

When the religious leaders of Jesus' day questioned Him about the greatest commandment of all, His response was set in today's verse:

> *The most important is, 'Hear, O Israel: The Lord our God, the Lord is one. And you shall love the Lord your God with all your heart and with all your soul and with all your mind and with all your strength.' The second is this: 'You shall love your neighbor as yourself.' There is no other commandment greater than these.* (Mark 12:30-31)

If Jesus proclaimed this truth, it would be wise for us to commit it to our memory.

The Week in Review!

Write this week's verse:

The thing(s) I'm most *grateful* for this week:
1.

2.

3.

How will I be **GRACIOUS** to others because of this week?

How will I be **GENEROUS** next week?

WEEK TWENTY-SEVEN

"Love your neighbor as yourself."
Matthew 22:39 NIV

I grew up in a relatively small rural town in North Carolina where everyone knew everyone. My best friend lived across the street from me, and it seemed like our entire world was within our immediate neighborhood. Everyone knew each other, cared for one another, and made sure that everyone was okay. If there was a problem with any of the neighborhood kids' behavior, it was certain that the on-site parent would correct and direct us immediately. There was an uncommon love between the folk of our neighborhood. Now, over 50 years later I can still travel back to that street of my childhood and have fond memories of that sense of community.

Neighborhoods have changed over the years and not necessarily for the better. Some have eroded into danger zones, while others have become so secure to feel like encampments. In either case, too often we have lost touch with those around us.

This week's scripture verse reminds us that Jesus summed up the great commands of God in two simple statements. Last week we learned that we are to "Love the Lord" completely. "After stating the first and greatest commandment, Jesus did the Pharisees one better and added *the second* as well: *You shall love your neighbor as yourself.* Not **surprisingly the second** greatest commandment involves the same virtue as the first, namely, **love**. The command for genuine love of God, Jesus declared, is next followed in importance by the command for a **love** of **your neighbor** that is of the same order as the love you already have for **yourself**."

Someone will ask, "Who is my neighbor?" The answer is not cloaked in mystery. The word used here implies someone who is "near, near to, close by, a fellow, another person of the same country, or any other member of the human family." In plan form, it means that person, right there. There is no case to be made for believing that only fellow believers are our neighbors. Whoever is around us has by definition become our neighbor.

The love that Jesus requires is far more than a mere sentimental or emotional feeling. This love is an intentional, personal, and active involvement in the lives of those around us. If we truly love God, we cannot but help love those around us. The Apostle John said this even more plainly:

> *Beloved, let us love one another, for love is from God, and everyone who loves is **born of God** and **knows** God. <u>The one who does not love does not know God</u>, for God is love.* (1 John 4:7-8)

Our great love for our neighbors is in knowing that they too are someone for whom Christ died. Our love for them is in wanting them to know and experience the love of God in Christ Jesus. The Apostle Paul wrote, *"Love does no wrong to a neighbor; love therefore is the fulfillment of the law"* (Romans 13:10).

"Love your neighbor as yourself!"

The Week in Review!

Write this week's verse:

The thing(s) I'm most *grateful* for this week:
1.

2.

3.

How will I be **GRACIOUS** to others because of this week?

How will I be **GENEROUS** next week?

WEEK TWENTY-EIGHT

"Do not be anxious about anything, but in every situation, by prayer and petition, with thanksgiving, present your requests to God. "
Philippians 4:6 NIV

In his book, *The Applause of Heaven*, Max Lucado describes the modern day "High D" personality:

> He's rich. Italian shoes. Tailored suit. His money is invested. His plastic is golden. He lives like he flies – first class. He's young. He pumps away fatigue at the gym and slam dunks old age on the court. His belly is flat, his eyes sharp. Energy is his trademark, and death is an eternity away. He's powerful. If you don't think so, just ask him. You got questions? He's got answers. You got problems? He's got solutions. You got dilemmas? He's got options. He knows where he's going, and he'll be there tomorrow. He's the new generation. So the old had better pick up the pace or pack their bags. He's mastered the three "P's" of yuppiedom, Prosperity, Posterity, Power. He's the rich ... young ... ruler.[20]

This man is headed for destruction. His life will only be a vapor if he doesn't slow down! In this day of the quick cash and the mad dash, we are seeing more and more people living in the Mess of Stress! Someone has observed that this generation can be described in three words: Hurry ... worry ... bury.

One commentator reported that:

> Americans are becoming hypochondriacs. We consume in the neighborhood of five million pounds of aspirin per year, not counting all the

aspirin-like products, plus sleeping pills, pain pills, and pep pills.

The American Heart Association estimates that 55 million American adults and 2.7 million children have high blood pressure. Certainly this is not as it should be. We live in a day of unprecedented stress and strain. There are thousands of self-help books on the market with winning ways of dealing with the Mess of Stress.

This week's verse talks about the right perspective we must have in the midst of trying and troubling times. The word "anxiety" translated is a reference to more than simple worry or frustration. It carries with it the idea of being overwhelmed, overcome, or controlled by something. It has an absoluteness to the worry. Yes, what Paul is warning against is the debilitating state that can come through the over consternation of circumstances.

Paul tells us clearly that we are to do three things when we find ourselves in times of trial:

Declare our faith. We must admit that we know that God holds all things together and is never caught off guard by our circumstances. *Don't be anxious at all.*

Describe our need. Never hesitate to talk to God about all that is troubling you. Talk plainly to Him as you would to your best friend. God alone is able to cause you to see clearly in the midst of your concern. *Go to God in prayer.*

Decide to trust. In every situation in life we make the choice to trust or forsake God. Make the deliberate determination to trust God in any and all situations. *Be thankful that God knows all things and hears our requests.*

The Week in Review!

Write this week's verse:

The thing(s) I'm most *grateful* for this week:
1.

2.

3.

How will I be **GRACIOUS** to others because of this week?

How will I be **GENEROUS** next week?

WEEK TWENTY-NINE

"And the peace of God, which surpasses all understanding, will guard your hearts and your minds in Christ Jesus."
Philippians 4:7 ESV

This week's verse is a continuation of Paul's instructions to the church at Philippi. The great love for this local congregation is obvious with each stroke of his pen. Having warned them to be "anxious for nothing," he now gives them the absolute assurance that it is possible and profitable for them to abide in a state of peace.

Peace is a misused and misunderstood word. A simple look at Webster's dictionary states that peace is "a state in which there is no war or fighting ... an agreement to end a war ... a period of time when there is no war or fighting."

For the sake of this week's study, I want to remind you that Paul has a much deeper meaning and understanding of the word "peace" than this. The beloved Apostle has just affirmed that because of God's complete control over everything and in light of the reality that God's purpose is always for our good, he exhorts his readers to live inside the "peace of God."

In his letter to the Romans Paul said plainly,

*Therefore having been justified by faith,
we have peace with God through our Lord Jesus Christ.*
(Romans 5:1)

This reminds us that once a person has been saved, he is no longer at war with God and can enjoy the peace of God in his daily life. The "peace of God" reminds us that He is in complete control over all. You and I do not have to struggle with keeping it all together because we have the internal assurance of knowing God.

While it is true that we may not always understand all that is going on in life, we have the assurance that nothing catches God off guard, and therefore we can abide in His peace. The ways of God are so far above human reason and understanding that we can never fathom the supremacy of God. Remember, the "peace of God" is supernatural and sufficient for every circumstance in which we find ourselves.

Not only does it surpass our understanding, it alone is able to guard our hearts and minds. Far too often we allow our head to get in the way of our heart. The word Paul uses for "guard" is a military word that means "as a soldier stands at a post" to protect a city. This is a picture that would have been very understandable to the city of Philippi where Roman soldiers were stationed to protect their treasures in that part of the world.

The good news of this week is that God's supernatural peace, which comes at conversion, is all we need to guard our hearts and minds. Thank God for that "peace" today!

The Week in Review!

Write this week's verse:

The thing(s) I'm most *grateful* for this week:
1.

2.

3.

How will I be **GRACIOUS** to others because of this week?

How will I be **GENEROUS** next week?

WEEK THIRTY

**"Every word of God proves true;
he is a shield to those who take refuge in him."**
Proverbs 30:5, ESV

I like to read. I enjoy a variety of genres, but my favorite casual reading comes in the form of historical fiction. While that sounds contradictory, it is not. I like books that are set in a historical context, but weave a story with characters which are fictional. My personal favorites are military and special ops books. While I am careful not to read them as battle proven, I enjoy the exercise.

The writer of Proverbs gives a stern warning to all who wish to mishandle the Word of God. Solomon writes that every word of God is "true or pure" by using the verb meaning "to refine or test. This word describes the purifying process of a refiner, who heats metal, takes away the dross, and is left with a pure substance."[21]

The word of God can be trusted and can always be put to the test. Regardless if we study the Bible as a whole or by individual parts, we will see that it is perfectly consistent in every way. While the Bible is not a work of history exclusively, when it speaks of history, it does so without error. It is not a book of science, but when it addresses scientific issues, it is true. When we read the Bible, we find it is inerrant, infallible, inspired, and infinite. It is the Word of God.

Far too many people approach the Bible with a bias toward it containing error. These skeptics have too low a view of God and too high a view of humanity. When the Bible comes in conflict with their own personal positions, they opt for their own understanding rather than accept that God's Word is perfect because it is

God's revelation of Himself to mankind. As the Baptist Faith & Message reminds us:

> *The Holy Bible...has God for its author, salvation for its end, and truth, without any mixture of error, for its matter. Therefore, all Scripture is totally true and trustworthy. It reveals the principles by which God judges us, and therefore is, and will remain to the end of the world, the true center of Christian union, and the supreme standard by which all human conduct, creeds, and religious opinions should be tried. All Scripture is a testimony to Christ, who is Himself the focus of divine revelation.*[22]

I hope you realize that as you are working on memorizing verses of scripture you are pouring into your heart and mind the very words of God which always point to the Lord Jesus Christ who is our shield in all of life. The Bible does not provide our salvation, but it does tell us the way to faith and belief through Jesus Christ.

From Genesis 1 through Revelation 22, we have the pure, true, tried, and tested Word of God that shows us the Lord Jesus. It's all true!

The Week in Review!

Write this week's verse:

The thing(s) I'm most *grateful* for this week:
1.

2.

3.

How will I be **GRACIOUS** to others because of this week?

How will I be **GENEROUS** next week?

WEEK THIRTY-ONE

"So whether you eat or drink or whatever you do, do it all for the glory of God."
1 Corinthians 10:31, NIV

I really like gadgets and I confess that I'm a sucker for the "As Seen On T.V." industry. A couple of years ago I was smitten by the **Pocket Hose Top Brass**.[23] This remarkable invention promised to be the last water hose I would ever need. Without hesitation I bought one and used it for the next two years.

While watering some plants that my wife Mary had recently set out, I discovered the truth about the hose. This "last hose I would ever need" suddenly burst through the outer casing and looked like a fully fed snake about to explode. I laughed it off and continued to water the shrubs. It was only another moment before it exploded, and my once "greatest gadget" had to be placed into the rubbish heap of fallen hopes.

One of the most common pitfalls of life is that we have an over-inflated view of ourselves and an under-inflated view of God. Too often fallen humanity assumes that our life is all about us and the things we want, crave, desire, and lust after. This egocentric view is solely based on the false sense of self-importance and self-sufficiency. Our overfilled egos will lead us to the rubbish heap of fallen hopes.

The absolute purpose of every human being is for us to glorify God. This is what living is all about. The Westminster shorter Catechism asks, "What is the chief end of man?" The answer is simple and concise. "Man's chief end is to glorify God and to enjoy him forever."[24] This week's scripture verse gives a simple reminder that we should do all things for the glory of God.

Someone might remark, "You don't know what my life looks like today," to which I reply, "but God does!" Any Christian who is living in discontent because of his job, his family, his finances, or any other thing, is living out a terrible testimony about the goodness of God. Is the God you serve sufficient for you in your circumstances?

Paul's constant theme of his writing is that every true child of God has the absolute assurance of His sovereignty, sufficiency, and supremacy in and through all things. Remember, as you memorize this verse of scripture that we can give glory to God through praise, persistence, and perseverance.

David wrote in Psalm 51:2, *"Restore to me the joy of Your salvation."* When we join him in this prayer, we are able to follow the instructions of Paul who wrote, "Whatever you do, do it to the glory of God."

The Week in Review!

Write this week's verse:

The thing(s) I'm most *grateful* for this week:
1.

2.

3.

How will I be **GRACIOUS** to others because of this week?

How will I be **GENEROUS** next week?

WEEK THIRTY-TWO

"In the beginning, God created the heavens and the earth."
Genesis 1:1 NIV

The simplest, yet most profound statement in all the Bible is this week's verse. This verse is not about the beginning of God but the foundational statement about creation. God is without beginning or end. He alone is eternal. Moses prayed, *"Before the mountains were born or you brought forth the earth and the world, from everlasting to everlasting, you are God"* (Psalm 90:2 NIV).

The fact that God created everything is certain even for those without belief. It might be good to think of this verse in this way, "When the beginning began to begin, God was." The Bible repeatedly declares that God is behind (and in front of) everything! Everything we know had a beginning. The universe – the heavens and the earth – is not eternal. The formation of all things did not just happen by chance. "There is a Creator – a Supreme Person, a Supreme Intelligence and Force – who created the universe, and the Creator has given the universe purpose and meaning."[25]

Genesis 1:1 is the bedrock of a Christian's worldview. "Whether conscious or subconscious, every person has some type of worldview. A personal worldview is a combination of all you believe to be true, and what you believe becomes the driving force behind every emotion, decision and action. Therefore, it affects your response to every area of life: from philosophy to science, theology and anthropology to economics, law, politics, art and social order — everything."[26]

Most people have a nonbiblical worldview, and the world itself constantly unleashes its demonic arsenal of attacks on a biblical worldview through television, movies, music, media, and academia. The enemy is never silent and is always seductive. All nonbiblical worldviews appeal to the flesh of humanity. It is very easy for Christians to incorporate the ideas of the flesh into our own personal lives.

John Phillips wrote:

> The first chapter of Genesis is one of the most God-centered chapters in the Bible. God is mentioned by name thirty-two times in thirty-one verses. Add to that the use of personal pronouns, and He is mentioned no less than forty-three times. Thus, on the very first page of Scripture the Holy Spirit brings us into the presence of God and keeps us there. No wonder Satan hates that chapter! No wonder he has brought up his heavy artillery to discredit it in the minds of men.[27]

It was God who created it all. Rest and rejoice in this wonderful proclamation!

The Week in Review!

Write this week's verse:

The thing(s) I'm most *grateful* for this week:
1.

2.

3.

How will I be **GRACIOUS** to others because of this week?

How will I be **GENEROUS** next week?

WEEK THIRTY-THREE

**"The heavens declare the glory of God;
the skies proclaim the work of his hands."**
Psalm 19:1 NIV

In the movie *Forrest Gump,* we get a glimpse into the complex life of a simple man. When reflecting on his time in Vietnam, Forrest said,

> Sometimes it would stop raining long enough for the stars to come out... and then it was nice. It was like just before the sun goes to bed down on the bayou. There was always a million sparkles on the water... like that mountain lake. It was so clear, Jenny, it looked like there were two skies one on top of the other. And then in the desert, when the sun comes up, I couldn't tell where heaven stopped and the earth began. It's so beautiful.[28]

I am sure you have your own experiences and examples of looking at the beauty of God's creation. There does not seem to be enough words to describe the beauty of a night sky.

I remember one night in Ghana when my ministry colleague, Mark Chase, and I were awed by the heavenly display of lights in the sky. The night was crystal clear and without any artificial lights but the majesty of God's glory was overwhelming. I think I had a glimpse of what David wrote in Psalm 8:

*O LORD, our Lord, How majestic is
Your name in all the earth. You have displayed Your
splendor above the heavens!*

Last week we were reminded that God is the creator of everything. In this week's verse we hear a hymn of praise from David as he reflects on the glory of God as revealed through nature.

The supreme God of all expects and demands praise. He can do this because He is God! Notice here that David says the heavens *declare* the glory of God. God's ways are above our ways and His glory cannot be overstated. God will always have His glory declared.

Jesus proclaimed to the religious crowd of His day that if people did not give Him the glory He deserved that even the "stones would cry out." You and I are given the responsibility and requirement to declare the glory of God through our words, works, witness, and worship. This requires us to live in the reality of His presence and power. This comes as we feast on the Word of God and choose to give Him all the glory.

I urge you to look to the sky and reflect on the marvelous, wondrous works of God. He is God and looks for your praise.

The Week in Review!

Write this week's verse:

The thing(s) I'm most *grateful* for this week:
1.

2.

3.

How will I be **GRACIOUS** to others because of this week?

How will I be **GENEROUS** next week?

WEEK THIRTY-FOUR

"The Lord knows the way of the righteous, but the way of the wicked will perish."
Psalm 1:6 ESV

The better translation of the Hebrew here would be "The Lord is *constantly knowing* the way of the righteous." We must always remember that God knows where we are and knows the way He has for us.

Several years ago while on a ministry project in Africa our team had an assignment which required us to cross the Volta Lake on a makeshift ferry boat. The adventure across was beautiful and fairly enjoyable. Once ashore in the Afram Plains district we had a very hot and dusty ride to our hotel where we learned that two of us had to travel further along the lake, which required both trucks and boats to get us to the assigned location for the evening.

The early evening sky was beginning to darken as we rode the trucks on rapidly declining roads which eventually became nothing more than a footpath that brought us to the water's edge. There we were met by another, much smaller boat which would be our passage across another part of the lake.

This boat was nothing more than a series of metal barrels lashed together by ropes and a few wooden planks laid over the barrels from side to side. On top of the deck the operator had positioned two long boards on which we were to drive our truck. He gave us a strict command to stay in the truck. Our mode of propulsion was a small outboard motor that sounded more like a chainsaw than a boat motor. By the time we set out the night sky was completely black, making the entire journey a bit eerie.

Getting the truck off the raft was challenging, but we did so and began to drive again to the end of the road where we got out and began to walk along a dark, uneven path. At least two of us stepped into ruts or holes and fell to the ground. I remember asking Sammy how could he possibly see where he was going on this hike.

His reply was a perfect connection with Psalm 1:6: "I have been on this path since I was just a child. I know the way because I have always been coming this way." Then he said, "Just stay in step with me and all will be well!"

From that moment on we never felt the slightest notion of being lost or in danger. Even through it was not a way I had been before, there was comfort in knowing that my guide knew it well. When the project was completed for that night, we retraced our steps, truck tracks, and voyages back to our hotel. By 2:30 am we were safe for a night's rest before our return to the same place the next morning for the dedication of a new church assembly from the evangelism efforts the night before. Somehow this second trip was far less adventurous because we had the confidence in knowing that our guide was "constantly knowing" the way.

As a child of God you have the absolute assurance that God *is knowing* the way He has planned for you. Stay in His steps and all will be well.

The Week in Review!

Write this week's verse:

The thing(s) I'm most *grateful* for this week:
1.

2.

3.

How will I be **GRACIOUS** to others because of this week?

How will I be **GENEROUS** next week?

WEEK THIRTY-FIVE

**"Thus says the LORD. Do not fear, for I have
redeemed you; I have called you by name;
you are mine!"**
Isaiah 43:1 NASB

Life is more of a marathon than a sprint. It is easy to
celebrate the pinnacles and curse the pitfalls. We are
filled with faith in the times of plenty but are filled with
fear in problematic times. We bless the mountaintops
and bane the valleys.

Denzel Washington once said, "You pray for rain, you
gotta deal with the mud too. That's a part of it."[29]

I kind of like that. It reminds me of one of the central
truths of God's word. God says, *"Do not fear ... I have
redeemed you ... you are mine!"* Contained within this
awesome verse we see the Proclamation, Provision, and
Promise of God to His children.

1. The **Proclamation is clear**: *"Do not fear."* This is not
    the announcement of another human being. It is not
    a word from simply someone who loves us, but it is
    from the One who created us. We are repeatedly
    instructed through God's word that fear is never the
    best thing for the child of God. Fear is the opposite
    of faith and faith is the gift of God. Therefore, *don't
    be afraid*!

2. The **Provision of God is convincing**: *"I have
    redeemed you."* The word "redeemed" is lost in our
    modern vocabulary. In Old Testament times
    everyone knew what it meant for a person to be
    redeemed. The word literally means "to buy back
    from bondage through a payment." This is exactly
    what God has done for all who believe.

Paul wrote the church in Ephesus, *"You were dead in your trespasses and sins ... But God, being rich in mercy, because of His great love with which He loved us, even when we were dead in our transgressions, made us alive together with Christ"* (Ephesians 2: 1,4-5a). God has redeemed us with a great price (1 Corinthians 6:20) – the free gift of God in Christ Jesus.

3. The **Promise of God is certain:** *"You are mine!"* Because we are His, we can be sure along with Paul who wrote, *"If God is for us, who can ever be against us? For I am convinced that nothing can ever separate us from God's love. Neither death nor life, neither angels nor demons, neither our fear for today nor our worries about tomorrow – not even the powers of hell can separate us from God's love ... indeed nothing in all creation will ever be able to separate us from the love of God that is revealed in Christ Jesus our Lord"* (Romans 8:31b,38,39b NLT).

The Week in Review!

Write this week's verse:

The thing(s) I'm most *grateful* for this week:

1.

2.

3.

How will I be **GRACIOUS** to others because of this week?

How will I be **GENEROUS** next week?

WEEK THIRTY-SIX

"I alone am the LORD, and there is no savior except me."
Isaiah 43:11 GWT

The single truth of God is summed up in this statement. God alone is God, and Jesus alone is the savior of the world.

Deep in the heart of every human is the desire to come to the end of their life and be accepted or approved by their god, whoever or whatever their god is. All the religions and philosophies of the world have as a certain tenet of their belief system the goal of getting to a position of peace.

Jesus Christ is the only Savior there is. *"Salvation is found in **no one else**, for there is no other name under heaven given to mankind by which we **must be saved**"* (Acts 4:12). When Jesus was born, the angel boldly announced, *"Unto you is born this day in the city of David a Savior who is Christ the Lord"* (Luke 2:11). Even here in Isaiah, the prophet is echoing and quoting God as saying, *"I, even I am the LORD; and beside me there is no Savior."*

Someone will say, "Well I believe that Jesus is *a way* to God, but not the *only way* to God." However, "man's belief or lack of belief in the *Saviourship* of Jesus does not change the fact that Jesus Christ is truly the *Saviour*. However, when a man recognizes that Jesus Christ is truly the *Saviour* and trusts Him to be *his Saviour,* then—and only then—does that man receive the benefits of Christ's saving power."[30]

When Jesus was with his disciples preparing them for his impending crucifixion, he spoke these comforting words to his beloved followers:

Do not let your heart be troubled; believe in God, believe also in Me. In My Father's house are many dwelling places; if it were not so, I would have told you; for I go to prepare a place for you. If I go and prepare a place for you, I will come again and receive you to Myself, that where I am, there you may be also. And you know the way where I am going." Thomas said to Him, "Lord, we do not know where You are going, how do we know the way?" Jesus said to him, "I am the way, and the truth, and the life; no one comes to the Father but through Me.
(John 14: 1-6 NASB)

Only Jesus promises and provides peace, because only Jesus is Lord and Savior.

The Week in Review!

Write this week's verse:

The thing(s) I'm most *grateful* for this week:
1.

2.

3.

How will I be **GRACIOUS** to others because of this week?

How will I be **GENEROUS** next week?

WEEK THIRTY-SEVEN

"You are the light of the world.
A city set on a hill cannot be hidden."
Matthew 5:14 ESV

There is something scary about the darkness. Parents know far too well what it means to go and look under the bed, in the closets, and behind the doors for their little ones. We assure those precious gifts of the Lord that nothing is there to "get them" and that we'll leave the night light on in the hall bathroom just to make sure.

I believe there is no place darker in all the world than India. I remember flying between cities in that country and realizing just what darkness was all about. No street lights, no car lights, no house lights, just darkness.

An old story is told of an Indian woman who walked home one night and was stalked by a panther. She carried a lantern and thus walked in a circle of light and was safe. She said, "The panther won't attack you while you are in the light. As long as you are in the light, you are safe from all attacks. Remember, always stay in the light."

Matthew 5:14 is a powerful affirmation from Jesus to his disciples, and thus to all believers. He does not say that his disciples will become the light of the world, rather he states that we ARE the light of the world. In John 8:12 Jesus makes this statement about himself, and thus as He is the light, we are most importantly reflectors of His light that resides in us.

As the sun is the physical light of the world, so Jesus (through us) is the spiritual light. As the sun makes objects visible and shows their true nature, beauty, and even deformities, so Christ shines His light on all people and reveals to them all that God intends, requires, expects, and demands of them.

The Light of the World shows us our true sinful condition and God's solution for our condition through the substitutionary death of Christ on the cross, his visible resurrection from the dead, and His complete victory over death, hell, and the grave. Once we have heard, seen, and received The Light, we are empowered with everything we need to face the realities of life.

It is good to remember that light does at least three things:

1. **Light *removes darkness.*** The light can never be overcome by the darkness. The smallest light in a dark place always chases the darkness away. In all of life we are challenged by the darkness of an evil and wicked world. I trust we will learn daily the advantage of walking in the Light of God's word.

2. **Light *reveals danger.*** I spend a great deal of time in Africa and have learned by experience that a flashlight is a very valuable part of my equipment. Too numerous are the times when an unknown danger was revealed and avoided because of the little flashlight. In the same way our physical, spiritual, and emotional lives are protected by the Light of God's word.

3. **Light *restores direction.*** It is easy for us to lose our way in moments of darkness, but the Light of God's word will always point us back to the path. I do not know what you are going through today, but I know that Jesus always shows you the way.

The Week in Review!

Write this week's verse:

The thing(s) I'm most *grateful* for this week:
1.

2.

3.

How will I be **GRACIOUS** to others because of this week?

How will I be **GENEROUS** next week?

WEEK THIRTY-EIGHT

"Let your light shine before men, that they may see your good deeds and praise your Father in heaven."
Matthew 5:16 ESV

What do people see in you? I read once about a man who stepped into a taxi and found the driver to be unusually friendly. Although this passenger was no stranger to taxis, he did find it unusual to have a driver so overwhelmingly cheerful, so he asked the man why he was so happy.

The driver replied, "It all started when I heard about another driver who was so kind to his passengers that one of his riders remembered his kindness and left him $65,000 in his will. I thought I would try it myself and that maybe one day someone would leave me something too. But after I tried it, I found it was so much fun being good that I decided I would do it for the fun of it, reward or no reward."

It is certainly better for us to be kind and gracious than not. Our motive, however, is not for the earthly rewards that might follow but for the praise of our Father in heaven.

If, however, you notice the world around you becoming darker and darker, don't blame the darkness! It is simply doing what darkness does. The only remedy for darkness is light. If the world is becoming darker, the problem is not with the darkness. The problem is with the light. Jesus said His disciples should be the *"light of the world"* (Matthew 5:14). What an awesome responsibility — to be the ones through whom God would shine His divine light and dispel the darkness from around others!

In announcing His own coming, Jesus said, *"The people who sat in darkness have seen a great light, and upon those who sat in the region and shadow of death, Light has dawned"* (Matthew 4:16).[31]

You and I have been given the great responsibility to reflect the Light of Jesus Christ through all our life. We are constantly having impact and influence on others. Admittedly not all of our impact or influence is positive, but it is always present.

Jesus says here that the purpose of letting our light shine and revealing our good works is not about bringing attention or applause to ourselves, but to God. The old Christian hymn says it simply:

> *While passing thro' this world of sin, and others your life shall view, Be clean and pure without, within; Let others see Jesus in you.*

> *Let others see Jesus in you, Let others see Jesus in you. Keep telling the story, be faithful and true; Let others see Jesus in you.*

> *Your life's a book before their eyes, They're reading it thro' and thro' Say, does it point them to the skies, Do others see Jesus in you?*

> *Then live for Christ both day and night, Be faithful, be brave and true, and lead the lost to life and Christ. Let others see Jesus in you.*[32]

I pray that others are seeing Christ in us today!

The Week in Review!

Write this week's verse:

The thing(s) I'm most *grateful* for this week:
1.

2.

3.

How will I be **GRACIOUS** to others because of this week?

How will I be **GENEROUS** next week?

WEEK THIRTY-NINE

"But seek first His kingdom and His righteousness, and all these things will be added to you."
Matthew 6:33 NASB

One of the most well-known sayings of the Navy SEALS is "**The only easy day was yesterday**." As we go through seemingly difficult times, we all come to know that the road ahead of us will continue to produce challenges, obstacles, and trials. Each of these are designed to remind us that God is fully capable and sufficient for all of our needs.

Jesus seems to give a single summary statement about the Christian life here in Matthew 6. Far too many people are overly worried, even anxious, about day-to-day living. Jesus never suggested that it's wrong for us to have thoughts or even concerns about our basic needs. He simply says that it is not necessary. Those outside the faith family can be gripped by frustration, anxiety, and uncertainties of life. For everyone who personally knows Jesus Christ as Lord and Savior, there is assurance about who holds today and tomorrow.

On this verse of scripture Oswald Chambers wrote:

> Get rightly related to God first, maintain that as the great care of your life, and never put the concern of your care on the other things. Jesus taught that a disciple has to make his relationship to God the dominating concentration of his life, and to be carefully careless about everything else in comparison to that. Jesus is saying, "Don't make the ruling factor of your life what you shall eat and what you shall drink, but be concentrated absolutely on God."[33]

The key to the Christian life is simple, but it is not easy.

Take golf for instance. I enjoy watching the majors each year — the Masters, the US Open, The Open Championship (British Open), and the PGA Championship. All these tournaments are fun to watch, and I am always amazed at the shots those professional golfers can make. Sitting in the comfort of my favorite chair I start to think, "I could make that shot" for, after all, what sport is more simple? I mean the ball is sitting still, I have complete control over the club in my hand and the target is easily identified. It's really a simple game, but when I get out on the course my perspective suddenly changes. I realize that while the game is SIMPLE, it certainly isn't EASY.

The same can be said of life in general and the Christian life specifically. Jesus summed up our game plan in simple words: *"Seek first the Kingdom of God..."* (Matthew 6:33 paraphrased). It's that simple, but it isn't that easy. We are easily distracted from this mandate. We are swept away by so many things that cry out for our attention. It requires a daily awareness of the fact that our life is not our own, but rather belongs to God and we need His guidance.

The great love that God has for us is evident in all of life. He cares more for you than you can comprehend. Seek His face and His direction in every aspect of your life. Use this exercise of memorizing scripture to fill your heart and mind with the Truth of Jesus Christ. In this way you are seeking Him!

The Week in Review!

Write this week's verse:

The thing(s) I'm most *grateful* for this week:
1.

2.

3.

How will I be **GRACIOUS** to others because of this week?

How will I be **GENEROUS** next week?

WEEK FORTY

"Let the word of Christ richly dwell within you."
Colossians 3:16a NASB

What does the word *home* mean to you? What picture comes to mind when you hear that word? Far too many people think of home as a house or a place to reside. Home for me is a state of relationship more than a state of residence. The ancient proverb says, "Home is where the heart is."

My father, born in 1921, joined the United States Navy just shy of his seventeenth birthday. He had been raised on a farm in North Carolina during the Great Depression and thus looked forward to the stability of serving in the Navy. He served through WWII and the Korean conflict, and was sunk twice during these years. He often told the stories of the times he would come home on leave. Each time he said his heart was thrilled at the thought of being back on that dirty farm and that small farmhouse, because it was *home.*

Paul writes in Colossians 3:16 *"Let the word of Christ dwell in your richly"* (NJKV). The word translated "dwell" means "to live in" or "to be at home." The author is instructing all true believers to allow the Word to take up residence and be at home in their lives. The word of Christ is simply the revelation that Christ brought into the world, which is Scripture. The truths of Scripture should impact, influence, and infiltrate every area of our life. John Phillips wrote,

> We need to get the Word out of our Bibles and into our hearts. The Word of Christ dwelling in our hearts becomes a vast treasury of wisdom upon which the Holy Spirit can draw as He guides us through the varying circumstances of life.[34]

One of the comforting yet challenging things about God's love for us is that He has given us absolute and confident access to everything He is and has for us. We have in our hands the very word of God which is sufficient for everything. The challenge is that the word of God will not flourish in a divided heart. Our heart is not designed to be a multifamily complex, but rather a single family place. Whatever is dividing our heart must be cleared out so that the word of Christ might dwell within us richly.

Consider these questions:

1. What is residing in my heart that needs to be cleared and cleaned out?

2. Am I willing to confess these things to the Lord and ask Him for His power to remove these from my heart?

3. Do I admit that He is sufficient to handle these things and replace them with His word?

4. Will I allow His word to take up residence and be at home in my heart today?

The Week in Review!

Write this week's verse:

The thing(s) I'm most *grateful* for this week:
1.

2.

3.

How will I be **GRACIOUS** to others because of this week?

How will I be **GENEROUS** next week?

WEEK FORTY-ONE

"Jesus Christ is the same yesterday and today and forever."
Hebrews 13:8 NASB

John Kehoe writes:

> In my courses, I teach the Law of Constant Change as a fundamental law of our life that needs to be both understood and harnessed if we are to have a happy and successful life. The Law states that everything in our life is in constant change, constantly in the process of becoming something else. *Nothing stays exactly as it is.* Nothing. Movement and change constitute the reality of our being.

> Our finances, our friendships, our career possibilities, our life opportunities, our health, our children, our parents, our daily activities, our insights, all are forever changing and becoming something else. To many, this is a frightening and daunting phenomenon, as most of us crave stability, *but stability is an illusion,* and you and your circumstances will change whether you like it or not, whether you want them to or not, because they cannot and will not remain the same."[35] (*emphasis mine*)

While certainly this is the position of humanity, the word of God declares something completely different. The writer of Hebrews (probably Paul) unashamedly pronounces that *"Jesus Christ is the same yesterday and today, and forever."* He is the unchangeable, unchanging, constant living word of God. Earlier in the book of Hebrews, we read,

*Your throne, O God, is forever and ever ...
in the beginning You, LORD (Christ) laid
the foundation of the of the earth, and the
heavens are the work of Your hands will
perish but You remain ...all of creation
will perish and change, but You (LORD)
are the same.* " (Hebrews 1:8, 10-12
paraphrased)

The truth of the matter is that even though all of
creation is in a state of constant flux and decline, we
have the absolute assurance that Jesus never – ever –
changes.

In theological circles this reality is known as the
immutability of God, which means His quality of not
changing. This is clearly taught throughout Scripture.
For example, in Malachi 3:6 God affirms, "I the Lord do
not change." (See also 1 Samuel 15:29; Isaiah 46:9-11;
and Ezekiel 24:14.)

The idea that Jesus is constantly in a state of flux blurs
the line that I think too many people ignore. Far too
often, in our constantly changing world, we have too
high a view of man and too low a view of God. Read
these words from Numbers 23:19:

*God is not man, that he should lie,
or a son of man, that he should change his mind.
Has he said, and will he not do it?
Or has he spoken, and will he not fulfill it?*

Yes, Jesus is the same yesterday and today and forever.

The Week in Review!

Write this week's verse:

The thing(s) I'm most *grateful* for this week:
1.

2.

3.

How will I be **GRACIOUS** to others because of this week?

How will I be **GENEROUS** next week?

WEEK FORTY-TWO

"Yet those who wait for the LORD will gain new strength; they will mount up with wings like eagles, they will run and not get tired, they will walk and not become weary."

Isaiah 40:31NASB

We live in a fast-paced society. Every day I speak with someone who is feeling overwhelmed with the circumstances of life. Perhaps you are feeling tired today. I want you to know that it is okay! All of us get tired. Maybe you have had a particularly difficult day, week, or month. Someone reading this is struggling with family, friends, faith, finances or something else. You are weary and worn and feel like you need some time of renewal and refreshment.

One of the privileges God has given me is the opportunity to talk with people from various walks of life on scheduled accountability calls or face-to-face meetings. Regardless of a person's profession, we all stand in need of some regular times of rejuvenation. Without a system of pressure release, we will always move toward wandering and drifting away from our desired place in life. Pressure will undeniably and unavoidably lead to stress, which will lead to fear, which will lead to anxiety, which will end in despair.

The key to dealing with this disaster is found in the first phrase of Isaiah 40:31, *"Yet those who wait for the* LORD..." Waiting upon the Lord is not a passive idea but rather an active, deliberate, and intentional state of mind. Don't think about waiting on the Lord as an idle time of twiddling your thumbs and whistling into the wind. You will discover that this time of waiting is perhaps the most active time in your spiritual life. There are at least three things that will transpire during this season of waiting:

1. You will **long** for the Lord. The Psalmist wrote,

As the deer pants for the water brooks, so my soul pants for Thee, O God. My soul thirsts for God, for the living God; when shall I come and appear before God?
(Psalm 42:1-2)

My soul waits in silence for God only; from Him is my salvation.
(Psalm 62:1)

2. You will **listen** to the Lord. Read the words of Solomon:

But he who listens to me shall live securely, and shall be at ease from the dread of evil. (Proverbs 1:33)

Blessed is the man who listens to me, watching daily at my gates, waiting at my doorposts. (Proverbs 8:34)

3. You will **look** to the Lord. Again the Psalmist writes,

They all wait for Thee, to give them their food in due season. Thou dost give to them, they gather it up; Thou dost open Thy hand, they are satisfied with good.
(Psalm 104: 27-28)

The eyes of all look to Thee, and Thou dost give them their food in due time. Thou dost open Thy hand, and dost satisfy the desire of every living thing.
(Psalm 145:15-16)

When we are waiting for the Lord, there is a time of desire (longing for the Lord), there is a time of devotion (listening to the Lord), and there is a time of direction (looking to the Lord). His promise is sure: He will give us new strength.

The Week in Review!

Write this week's verse:

The thing(s) I'm most *grateful* for this week:
1.

2.

3.

How will I be **GRACIOUS** to others because of this week?

How will I be **GENEROUS** next week?

WEEK FORTY-THREE

**"Peace I leave with you; my peace I give you.
I do not give to you as the world gives. Do not let
your hearts be troubled and do not be afraid."**
John 14:27NIV

Have you ever been persecuted for your faith? The Bible guarantees persecution for the child of God, and it can manifest itself in many different ways and in varying degrees. You may have been laughed at, ridiculed, or derided in some fashion, but have you ever been persecuted to the point of being prohibited from practicing and professing your faith? What about to the point of physical harm or the threat of death?

Suppose armed gunmen burst through your church's door demanding a halt to the worship service? What would be your response? Suppose the President declared it a capital offense to possess a Bible, pray a prayer, or speak a word of testimony to another person. How would you deal with that circumstance?

Indeed, it is incredible to think that these types of scenarios can actually happen today. We may not be able to conceive of these things occurring in America, but we can let history of the past as well as prophecy of the future be a guide to our thinking.

Persecution unto death has certainly been a fact of the past – at the founding of the Christian church in the first century, under Adolph Hitler in the early 20th century – and it has not been abolished in the present. Concerning the future, the Bible clearly states the coming of tribulations resulting in mass murders of people due to their faith.

While we cannot be insulated in our thinking about the past and the far distant future, we certainly should not be complacent concerning the present. More Christians have been killed for their faith in Jesus Christ in the last 100 years than the previous 1,900 years combined. We should not find ourselves ignorant, indifferent, or silent about this persecution. Even today in some Muslim countries Christians are dragged out of the homes, hanged on gallows, stoned, beheaded, and crucified. Profession to follow Jesus Christ is illegal in some places around the world.

As Jesus talked to His disciples in John 14, the context shows that their world was about to fall apart. Jesus was headed for the cross. The betrayer, Judas Iscariot, had already left their company and was planning his dirty deed in the dark of night. As these remaining disciples gathered around Jesus, He promised them a peace beyond compare. In all their encounters with the son of God they had witnessed an indescribable peace despite the demands of life or the threats from His enemies. This is the peace He promised them.

The Bible teaches that fearing man brings snares and trusting in mankind ends with destruction. Jesus promises His peace even in the midst of troubles and persecution and it is wholly different than the pretended peace offered by the world. Throughout history nations and peoples have talked about peace as they prepare for war. The world will never know peace because the world is under the direction of the enemy.

The peace Jesus gives passes all understanding and is the precious promise to a believer yielded to His Spirit. It is a promise for the here and now and forevermore. If you have peace with God, take care that you keep the peace of God – both found only in Jesus Christ.

The Week in Review!

Write this week's verse:

The thing(s) I'm most *grateful* for this week:
1.

2.

3.

How will I be **GRACIOUS** to others because of this week?

How will I be **GENEROUS** next week?

WEEK FORTY-FOUR

**"Delight yourself also in the LORD, and
He shall give you the desires of your heart."**
Psalm 37:4 NKJV

Do you remember the first job you ever wanted? I'm not talking about your carefully thought out career path, I mean the first job you thought would be cool, fun, exciting, and adventurous. Perhaps you wanted to be a cowboy, an army man, or an explorer.

I can remember, like it was yesterday, the day I thought I had found the most perfect job in the world. I wanted to be a "garbage picker upper!" As I watched these men come through our neighborhood to collect the trash, it was so great because they had the chance to hang off the back of the big truck as it weaved its way through our streets. That had to be the coolest thing ever!

My next desire exchanged the garbage man for an astronaut when in July of 1969 Neil Armstrong said, "that's one small step for man, one giant leap for mankind." Needless to say, I never actually became an astronaut.

The Psalmist here gives us absolute assurance that God will give us the desires of our heart as we delight in Him. To delight means to be soft and pliable in the Lord. Most of us get our desire in front of our delight. We look for, think about, even dream about something we want to do or become and set about doing everything we can to accomplish that goal. We spend vast amounts of time, talent, and treasures in the pursuit of our desires. This is the natural way of fallen man. We tend to run out ahead of God instead of resting and waiting on Him (v7).

God's way offers the exact opposite activity in the fulfillment of our desires. The Bible says clearly we are to trust in the Lord, commit our way to the Lord, and delight in the Lord first. C. H. Spurgeon wrote,

> Our foolish way is to desire, and then set to work to compass what we desire. We do not go to work in God's way, which is to seek Him first, and then expect all things to be added unto us. If we will let our heart be filled with God till it runs over with delight, then the Lord Himself will take care that we shall not want any good thing. He can do for us far more than all our friends. It is better to be content with God alone than to go about fretting and pining for the paltry trifles of time and sense. For a while we may have disappointments; but if these bring us nearer to the Lord, they are things to be prized exceedingly, for they will in the end secure to us the fulfillment of all our right desires.[36]

The more intimate we become with the Lord, our desires will be His desires. Delight in Him today.

The Week in Review!

Write this week's verse:

The thing(s) I'm most *grateful* for this week:
1.

2.

3.

How will I be **GRACIOUS** to others because of this week?

How will I be **GENEROUS** next week?

WEEK FORTY-FIVE

"Ask, and you will receive, that your joy may be full."
John 16:24b NKJV

The telephone rang and the voice on the other end was in an obvious place of turmoil. Nothing was going as planned and she was desperate for some reassurance and help.

Oswald Chambers wrote,

> There is nothing more difficult than asking. We will have yearnings and desires for certain things, and even suffer as a result of their going unfulfilled, but not until we are at the limit of desperation will we ask ... Yet we will never receive if we ask with a certain result in mind, because we are asking out of our lust, not out of our poverty. A pauper does not ask out of any reason other than the completely hopeless and painful condition of his poverty. He is not ashamed to beg — blessed are the paupers in spirit (see Matthew 5:3).[37]

It is not until we come to the end of ourselves that we have the inclination to ask. Friends, it ought not be so for the child of God.

My sweet wife and I enjoy playing golf together. Several years ago she clearly communicated with me that she neither wanted nor needed me to tell her anything about her golf swing. She repeatedly reminded me, "Don't tell me what I'm doing wrong!" I heeded her words.

On one particular day we were playing on a beautiful course in the mountains of North Carolina. The views were incredible, the course was impeccable, and the difficulty was irritating. The rolling terrain was certainly taking its toll on Mary. After a particularly challenging hole, she looked at me and asked, "What am I doing wrong?" I was a bit perplexed and found myself in a muddle. Despite my previous instructions and after giving her request instantaneous consideration, I found myself giving her one quick adjustment thought and she hit the ball longer, straighter, and more accurately than she had all day long.

The point of this illustration is certainly not about my ability to coach someone on their golf swing! Those who have played golf with me know how absolutely unqualified I am to do any such thing! The point is that it was only when Mary came to the place of desperation and helplessness that she was willing to ask for and accept instruction.

The same principle is at work in our spiritual lives. Far too often we think that we can handle almost anything that comes our way. We are living in a world of chaos that seems to be devoid of answers, but Jesus IS the answer! The context of John 16 is the promise of Jesus' finished work on the cross and His effectual resurrection. This glorious work gives direct access to the Father in prayer to all believers in the Son. The Son of God is urging His followers to *"ask and you will receive* [in order] *that your joy may be made* [completely] *full."*

Because of Jesus' atoning work on the cross and victorious resurrection from the grave we have the absolute confidence of knowing that all we have to do is ask, as long as we ask according to His prompting and will. "Answered prayer, based on the finished work of Jesus Christ and springing from an obedient life (15:10-11), is a powerful force in turning sorrow into joy."[38] Go ahead... ASK.

The Week in Review!

Write this week's verse:

The thing(s) I'm most *grateful* for this week:
1.

2.

3.

How will I be **GRACIOUS** to others because of this week?

How will I be **GENEROUS** next week?

WEEK FORTY-SIX

"For God so loved the world that He gave His only begotten Son, that whosoever believes in Him should not perish but have everlasting life.
John 3:16 NKJV

The entirety of the Gospel is encapsulated in John 3:16, which is the most quoted and memorized verse in all the Bible. No other statement from the Bible so perfectly summarizes God's redemptive plan and purpose in Christ for humanity. So many books have been written on this verse and yet there is more to say about this statement than there are words available.

The context of the verse comes on the heels of a conversation that Jesus had with an extremely religious man by the name of Nicodemus. The scripture tells us that he was a Pharisee and a *"ruler of the Jews."* He was strict about keeping the Mosaic law: the Sabbath, tithing, circumcision, ceremonial cleanliness, eating the right food, and observing holy days.

The title of ruler is often used in rabbinic literature for a "great man" or "prince." John Phillips notes, "Rabbinical tradition makes Nicodemus one of the three richest men in Jerusalem."[39] He was a champion of the religious community, yet he apparently did not know how to have a personal relationship with God. This is seen in his confusion over the statement that Jesus made: *"Unless one is born again, he cannot see the kingdom of God"* (John 3:3).

Since the fall of the human race in the garden of Eden (Genesis 3), mankind has been in search for a way into relationship with holy God. Yet because all humanity is completely lost, utterly sinful, and incapable of redeeming, saving, or bettering itself by religious ceremony or human effort, we are thus hopeless and helpless. The good news expressed in John 3:16 is that God loved the fallen world with an incomprehensible and gracious love displayed through His Son, the Lord Jesus Christ!

Paul wrote, *"But God demonstrates His own love toward us, in that while we were still sinners, Christ died for us"* (Romans 5:8 NKJV).

Try reading this week's verse through ten times, meditatively. With each reading put the emphasis on a different word. "For **God** so loved the world, that He gave his only begotten Son, that whosoever believeth in Him should not perish, but have everlasting life." Then: "For God so **loved** the world, that He gave his only begotten Son, that whosoever believeth in Him should not perish, but have everlasting life." Next: "For God so loved the **world**, that He gave..." And so on. The result will be ten meaningful meditations. The text is inexhaustible. All the highways of divine truth meet in this metropolis. It is the hub of all revealed truth.[40]

If you commit to memory only one verse, this should be it. This verse contains all the rich truth that is sufficient for every moment of every day. Read it. Memorize it. Know it. Believe it. Share it.

The Week in Review!

Write this week's verse:

The thing(s) I'm most *grateful* for this week:
1.

2.

3.

How will I be **GRACIOUS** to others because of this week?

How will I be **GENEROUS** next week?

Week Forty-Seven

"Beloved, let us love one another, for love is from God; and everyone who loves is born of God and knows God.
1 John 4:7 NASB

Last week we read about the great love with which God has loved us (John 3:16) and this week the same writer pens these words about love. As Paul wrote his great love poem in 1 Corinthians 13, this seems to be John's hymn of love. This single verse he tells us who we should love.

One of the most misunderstood words in the English language is love. By definition love is:

- an intense feeling of deep affection
- a deep romantic or sexual attachment to someone
- a personified figure for love
- a great interest and pleasure in something

The problem with the English language is that we use the same word for all of the above listed meanings. We say that we **love** our wife and then we say we **love** ice cream. We know that these two uses of the word have different meanings, but the language does not distinguish the two.

The word used for love in 1 John 4:7 is very specific and targeted. Unlike emotional, physical, or the friendship kind of love that the world knows of, it is the Greek word *agape* that John is describing here – a love of self-sacrificing service that is given to someone who needs to be loved, and not necessarily to one who is immediately lovable. This kind of love is that which exists and is known only through God.

The impetus for this instruction is for all believers to love one another. The very idea that John found it necessary to include this instruction in his book reveals the continued decline of humanity. It should be obvious to the redeemed that we should love all who have been redeemed. Oftentimes we act counter to John's instructions. We hear such unkind words coming from the mouths of Christians with regards to other Christians. I read somewhere that Vance Havner is credited with saying, "The church has never suffered so much from woodpeckers on the outside as from termites on the inside!"

Our great witness to the world should be the love that we show for one another. John says that we who are the divinely loved ones – those who have been redeemed by the blood of Jesus – are to be the beloved. He is restating that all true love is from God alone. The very idea that we can generate love of our own volition is ridiculous. Within our own capacities it is unnatural for us to love the unlovely. Our flesh is always looking for something in return. We are more interested in our needs that the needs of others. The great truth of this passage is that we have been loved by God and that love has been perfected in Jesus Christ.

John's simple, yet profound statement is this: God is love and His love resides in your life, therefore we are to love others.

This is the proof that you know God. eve it. Share it.

The Week in Review!

Write this week's verse:

The thing(s) I'm most *grateful* for this week:
1.

2.

3.

How will I be **GRACIOUS** to others because of this week?

How will I be **GENEROUS** next week?

WEEK FORTY-EIGHT

**"*Let us think of ways to motivate one another
to acts of love and good works.*"**
Hebrews 10:24 NLT

For the third week in a row our verse of scripture has at its heart the word love. Not only are we to love God and others, but now we discover the admonition to encourage others.

In a challenge-filled world it is easy for us to lose sight of doing the basics. Each person, of course, defines and determines these basics. Often it is in the midst of seemingly good times that we become slack and complacent in doing the things we know we need to do.

I have a friend who is better at the basics than anybody I know because he has suffered the consequences too often of letting the basics slip. Ever since his last major stumble, he has become a creature of habit. This guy eats the same breakfast and lunch every day. He is regimented about going to the gym the same days each week. He follows the same routine every afternoon. His days are rigidly scheduled and his life is structured like no one else I know.

I have another friend who is similarly structured but only when the things in his life are in a state of chaos. Every time we talk I am able to tell, nearly immediately, if he is in a delightful or difficult place in his life. The more trouble this guy is in the more diligent he is at getting back to the basics. He is circumstantially controlled and knows the right thing to do, but does not often do it. James wrote, *"Therefore, to one who knows the right thing to do and does not do it, to him it is sin"* (James 4:17).

My friend's real problem is that he seems to think that the activity of serving God is some sort of placebo for God's blessings.

A part of the human mind is to realize that we are all creatures of habit – some good, some bad, and some neutral. The writer of Hebrews admonishes us to *"think of **ways to motivate** [or stir up] one another ..."* to love and to good works. While it is easy for us to provoke people in the wrong ways, here the author is telling us to find ways that emphasize the Divine attributes of love and good in them. Here are a few things I think might help you in this:

Maximize victories and minimize failures. Too often we are quick to point out the failures in others rather than encourage them in the small victories in their lives. There certainly is a time and place for correction in our friends' lives but we must gain the opportunity to speak these more deliberate words to them through a developed relationship with them.

Be gracious in your choice of words. The old adage, "You can catch more flies with honey than with vinegar" is certainly true. People tend to listen more quickly through gentle and gracious words than they do through hostile confrontation. Think of your own experiences and share these with others.

Always be vulnerable with other people. Let your life be an open book for others to see. As we encourage others, it is important for them to see that we have been through many of the same things they are facing. As God has dealt with you so deal with others.

This week, I hope you will be constantly thinking of ways to motivate others to a good and godly life.

The Week in Review!

Write this week's verse:

The thing(s) I'm most *grateful* for this week:
1.

2.

3.

How will I be **GRACIOUS** to others because of this week?

How will I be **GENEROUS** next week?

WEEK FORTY-NINE

"Finally, brothers, whatever is true, whatever is honorable, whatever is just, whatever is pure, whatever is lovely, whatever is commendable, if there is any excellence, if there is anything worthy of praise, think about these things."
Philippians 4:8 NIV

The devil works hard to get our minds into the wrong places. The Enemy aggressively wants and waits for us to give in to his attacks because he wants our feelings to force us into wrong actions when the truth is that God wants our right actions to change our minds into new feelings. All of us know that our mind is a battlefield of our life.

Last week we looked at Hebrews 10: 24 – *"Let us think of ways to motivate one another to acts of love and good works."* This verse clearly stated that the subject of our thoughts is important. This week we have more clarity into how that subject is to be formulated.

I remember one of the first things I learned when I was taking a class on how to operate a computer was the acronym GIGO (Garbage In, Garbage Out). I think it applies to much more than just computer programming. You have heard me put it this way, "Whatever is in the well comes up in the bucket." The writer of Proverbs wrote *"For as he thinks within himself, so he is"* (Proverbs 23:7).

Paul sets our design for thinking out clearly and concisely by starting with the word **true**. Paul knew, as Jesus taught, that the Word of God is truth. When we think on what is true, we are basing our thoughts on the Word of God. As we think, meditate, contemplate, and act on the Word of God, we will be directed in our words and deeds.

The next thing Paul says in our verse is that our thought should be based on what is **honorable,** which means noble, dignified, and worthy of respect. In other words, there are some things in life that are unworthy of our attention and thoughts. Paul then moves us into a seamless thread of thought like this. Think about those things that are **just pure lovely**! Think of these words for what they actually say. Don't look for the deeper theological meaning here, just accept them on face value.

Paul ties this tapestry together by declaring "**whatever is commendable**" (or of good repute), think on these things! He is imploring with us to think on the most excellent and lofty themes of God's grace should be the subject of every believer's thoughts. When we think rightly, we will be able to speak more correctly.

Perhaps today we should utilize the THINK test before we speak by asking:

T   is it TRUE?
H   is it HELPUL?
I   is it IMPORTANT?
N   is it NESESSARY?
K   is it KIND?

If your words don't pass the THINK test, then don't speak them!

The Week in Review!

Write this week's verse:

The thing(s) I'm most *grateful* for this week:
1.

2.

3.

How will I be **GRACIOUS** to others because of this week?

How will I be **GENEROUS** next week?

WEEK FIFTY

"As iron sharpens iron, so one man sharpens another."
Proverbs 27:17 NASB

I grew up in an era where every boy and man carried a pocketknife. If I had my pants on, I had a knife. I took it to school during the week and to church on the weekend. I always had my pocketknife. Those days have been replaced by an era where those little knives are seen as weapons of mass destruction! I have had more fun watching the TSA officers in airports discover one of these little knives in people's luggage as they tried to make it through the security line.

I have spent a considerable amount of time over the past sixteen years in West Africa. Of all the things I have needed in the field, few, if any, are more necessary than my pocketknife. I use it almost every day while I am on a project. One of the difficulties while there is keeping it sharp.

I remember one specific time when I needed a sharp knife and only had my dull and useless CRKT. After trying everything I knew to do to sharpen this knife, I turned in desperation to my local friend named Simon and asked for his help. I thought he would be able to find me a stone to use but he simply asked if he could keep my knife for a little while.

The next time a saw Simon, just a couple of hours later, he handed me my newly sharpened knife with a smile. I don't remember ever seeing it that sharp and I asked him how he'd done it. His reply was priceless. "I used the word of God," he said with a smile. "Proverbs 27:17 tells me that 'iron *sharps* iron,' so I found a piece of iron and I *sharped* it."

This verse of scripture, while literally true, is also figuratively true. Just as surely as the rubbing together of two metal blades brings sharper edges which enables the knives to be more efficient and useful, so the continual fellowship of mutual brothers strengthens, encourages, and sharpens them.

It is imperative that Christians surround themselves with other Christians. We are mutually akin and identical because of the Spirit of Christ abiding within us. We are new creations through His transforming, saving, and sanctifying work in us. The same Spirit lives within all true believers, but the fact is that not everyone hears identically from the Spirit individually. It is often in our times of struggles, frustrations, and turmoil that we more willingly hear the Spirit's words through another believer. While this is completely a problem for the unyielding and unhearing person and in no way a problem with the Spirit, it is comforting to know that God continues to speak to and draw us unto Himself.

The absolute truth is that our conversations with other believers in times of sharpening must be with the Word of God. While it is easy to interject our opinion in the matters of life, the only certainty for truth is found in the Word of God. Too often what the Christian world refers to as fellowship, sadly even in the local church, comes in the form of meals and movies. The truest fellowship comes as we gather around the Word of God and achieve unity of the Spirit. The Psalmist wrote, *"How good and pleasant it is for brothers to dwell together in unity"* (Psalms 133:1!)

As we dwell in this unity, we will certainly be in the best position to sharpen one another.

The Week in Review!

Write this week's verse:

The thing(s) I'm most *grateful* for this week:

1.

2.

3.

How will I be **GRACIOUS** to others because of this week?

How will I be **GENEROUS** next week?

Week Fifty-One

"Cast all your anxiety on Him because He cares for you."
1Peter 5:7 NIV

Most parents have a similar story. We travel with our children to a park or zoo or an amusement park looking for a fun-filled day of activities only to discover that eventually the little legs of the youngster seem to no longer be able to carry their own weight. After several whines or complaints, the adult does the natural thing of hoisting the child onto their back or shoulders to carry them for the next leg of the journey.

I remember a very specific day in my own life when our four-year old grandson could walk no further and pled, "Pop-Pop, can I ride on your back, my legs don't work anymore?" I tossed the little guy on my shoulders and carried him along. It was a burden I was willing to bear because he was my grandchild. Within a few moments, he was fast asleep, knowing that he was free of the worry and at peace on Pop-Pop's shoulders.

It is a similar picture that Peter paints in this week's scripture verse. The original recipients of Peter's letter certainly knew something about the cares of the world. John Phillips wrote, "How many cares there were in that old pagan world, where God's beloved people were hated, hunted, and hurt at the demented will of a demonic tyrant!" It is against this backdrop that Peter simply instructs them to cast their cares upon Jesus.

The word he uses for **cast** occurs only one other time in scripture. Luke wrote that the disciples **cast** their garments on the back of the colt to make a saddle for Jesus to sit upon as he rode into Jerusalem (Luke 19:35). The clear implication is that we should not hold on to those things but rather lay them aside. While we tend to resist this process as difficult or complex, Peter is saying it's really very simple – take the initiative to let the care go and lay it down! It is just like getting rid of a dusty garment by willingly (and joyfully) tossing it on to the back of the colt. No matter what you are facing today, you do not have to continue to carry it, just cast it upon Jesus.

Anxieties will arise in our life but we are not to bear with them. God admonishes us not to worry about anything! It is both foolish and arrogant to believe that we are suited to handle the anxieties of life within ourselves. One of the great manifestations of God's grace is in the assurance of Peter's affirmation, "because He cares for you." The word used here indicates the kind of care that comes from *"having an interest in someone."*

I am certain that Peter could remember the teachings of Jesus regarding anxiety and the illustrations from the natural world about how the Heavenly Father took care of them.

In all of life's complexities we can be sure that God has an interest in us. The truth of the gospel is the fact that we have offended our Creator through sin and are thus deserving of hell, but God has graciously and generously given His Son and through Him purchased a full and free redemption that is received through repentance and faith. Our pardon and forgiveness He has proclaimed for all eternity. He cares that much! *"Cast all your cares upon Him because He cares for you!"*

The Week in Review!

Write this week's verse:

The thing(s) I'm most *grateful* for this week:
1.

2.

3.

How will I be **GRACIOUS** to others because of this week?

How will I be **GENEROUS** next week?

WEEK FIFTY-TWO

"Let everything that has breath praise the Lord. Praise the Lord!"
Psalm 150:6 NASB

The book of Psalms begins and ends in blessing. In the beginning we see how God blesses man, and in the end we see man blessing God. This final stanza of the Psalms beckons like a conductor before his orchestra and choir with one final admonition. *"Praise the Lord!"*

The Author of all creation has given us, through His infallible Word, our instruction and invitation to show Him absolute honor and glory through our praise. The Psalmist is saying that our breath should praise God because God alone gave us breath, and we have the very nature of God within us.

Read again the words of Genesis 2:7: *"Then the Lord God formed man of dust from the ground, and* **breathed** *into his nostrils the* **breath** *of life; and man became a living being."*

It should not come as a surprise that the breath of life should breathe out praise and adoration to God.

When Jesus made His triumphal entry into Jerusalem on the first Palm Sunday, the *"crowd of disciples praised God joyfully with a loud voice"* (Lk.19:28-39) and when religious leaders of that day confronted Jesus by telling Him that He should rebuke these disciples for ascribing praise and blessings to Him, his response reminded us that God will always be praised.

"But Jesus answered, I tell you if these become silent, the stones will cry out" (Luke 19: 40)!

The great joy of knowing Christ means that the redeemed do not have to wait until all creation stands before the Divine Judge to lavish praise on Him. One day *every knee will bow and every tongue will confess that Jesus is Lord* (Philippians 2:9-11) but rather now while we breathe on earth we can praise Him for Who He is, what he has done, what He is doing, and what He will do.

Gregory of Nyssa says,

> All creatures, after the disunion and disorder caused by sin have been removed, are harmoniously united for one choral dance, and the chorus of mankind concerting with the angel chorus are become one cymbal of divine praise, and the final song of victory shall salute God, the triumphant Conqueror, with shouts of joy.

Let this page and all pages everywhere end with these words, ***"Praise the Lord!"***

The Week in Review!

Write this week's verse:

The thing(s) I'm most *grateful* for this week:
1.

2.

3.

How will I be **GRACIOUS** to others because of this week?

How will I be **GENEROUS** next week?

Endnotes and References

[1] http://www.movemequotes.com/top-50-be-thankful-quotes/

[2] Complete Word Study Dictionary, The - The Complete Word Study Dictionary – Old Testament.

[3] John Phillips, The John Phillips Commentary Series, Exploring Proverbs, Vol. 1

[4] John MacArthur, Jr., The MacArthur New Testament Commentary, 1&2 Thessalonians

[5] http://www.christnotes.org/commentary.php?com=mhc&b=46&c=16

[6] Bible Exposition Commentary - Bible Exposition Commentary – Be Complete (Colossians).

[7] http://itmanagersinbox.com/1559/how-passion-for-your-job-can-lead-to-success/

[8] http://www.biblestudytools.com/dictionaries/bakers-evangelical-dictionary/heart.html

[9] MacArthur New Testament Commentary, The - MacArthur New Testament Commentary – Philippians.

[10] Margaret Thatcher. (ned). BrainyQuote.com. Retrieved January 15, 2016, from BrainyQuote.com Web site: http://www.brainyquote.com/quotes/quotes/m/margaretth382871.html

[11] https://en.wikipedia.org/wiki/I_Heard_the_Bells_on_Christmas_Day

[12] John Phillips Commentary Series, The - The John Phillips Commentary Series – Exploring the Epistle of James: An Expository Commentary.

[13] MacArthur New Testament Commentary, The - MacArthur New Testament Commentary – Galatians.

[14] John Phillips Commentary Series, The - The John Phillips Commentary Series – Exploring Psalms, Volume One: An Expository Commentary.

[15] MacArthur New Testament Commentary, The - MacArthur New Testament Commentary – 1 & 2 Thessalonians.

[16] https://www.biblegateway.com/passage/?search=2+Timothy+1%3A7-9&version=DARBY

[17] Complete Word Study Dictionary, The - The Complete Word Study Dictionary New Testament.

[18] Bible Exposition Commentary - Bible Exposition Commentary – Be Exultant (Psalms 90-150).

[19] John Phillips Commentary Series, The - The John Phillips Commentary Series – Exploring Psalms, Volume Two: An Expository Commentary.

[20] Max Lucado, The Applause of Heaven, Thomas Nelson, 1990.

[21] Complete Word Study Dictionary, The - The Complete Word Study Dictionary – Old Testament.

[22] http://www.lifeway.com/lwc/files/lwcF_PDF_BaptistFaithMesageSample.pdf

[23] http://www.pockethosetopbrass.com/?gclid=CM_3zZyGqswCFdgSgQodWPQGjw

[24] http://www.reformed.org/documents/wsc/index.html?_top=http://www.reformed.org/documents/WSC.html

[25] The Preacher's Outline & Sermon Bible, Alpha-Omega Ministries, Inc. Database 2013 WORD*search*

[26] http://www.focusonthefamily.com/faith/christian-worldview/whats-a-christian-worldview/whats-a-worldview-anyway

[27] John Phillips Commentary Series, The - The John Phillips Commentary Series – Exploring Genesis: An Expository Commentary.

[28] http://www.imdb.com/character/ch0002102/quotes

[29] Denzel Washington. BrainyQuote.com, Xplore Inc, 2016.

[30] Handbook of Personal Evangelism

[31] Experiencing God Day by Day: A Devotional and Journal.

[32] http://www.hymnlyrics.org/requests/let_others_see_jesus_in_you.php

[33] My Utmost for His Highest.

[34] John Phillips Commentary Series, The - The John Phillips Commentary Series – Exploring Colossians & Philemon: An Expository Commentary.

[35] http://www.learnmindpower.com/articles/law-constant-change/ - sthash.wib4jWw8.dpuf

[36] Faith's Checkbook, C.H. Spurgeon, November 6

[37] http://utmost.org June 9, 2016

[38] MacArthur New Testament Commentary, The - MacArthur New Testament Commentary – John 12-21.

[39] John Phillips Commentary Series, The - The John Phillips Commentary Series – Exploring the Gospel of John: An Expository Commentary.

[40] Ibid

About the Author

Photo by Michael Johnson

Dr. Roy D. Mason, Jr., has been in full-time Christian ministry since 1980, serving as pastor in five different churches in North Carolina. In 2001, after 20 years in local church ministry, he launched out in faith and began an international evangelistic endeavor which has allowed him to share the gospel in 16 countries with more than 1,000,000 people.

Growing up in the home of a retired Naval officer taught Roy the importance of honor, courage, commitment, and loyalty.

Roy's formal education includes a bachelor of science in pastoral studies from Campbell University, and both a masters of theology and a doctor of ministry from Bethany Theological Seminary.

Dr. Mason married his sixth-grade classmate Mary in 1978, and they have two grown daughters and four grandchildren. The bond between Pop-Pop and his two grandsons is incredible, and they know they are his best friends.